Dips, Tips & Poker Chips

Copyright © 2005 CQ Products
Waverly, IA 50677
All rights reserved.
No part of this book may be reproduced or transmitted in any form or by
any means, electronic or mechanical, including photocopying, recording
or by any information storage and retrieval system, without permission in
writing from the publisher.

Printed in the United States of America
by G&R Publishing Co.

Distributed By:

507 Industrial Street
Waverly, IA 50677

ISBN-13: 978-1-56383-220-8
ISBN-10: 1-56383-220-8
Item #7012

Table of Contents

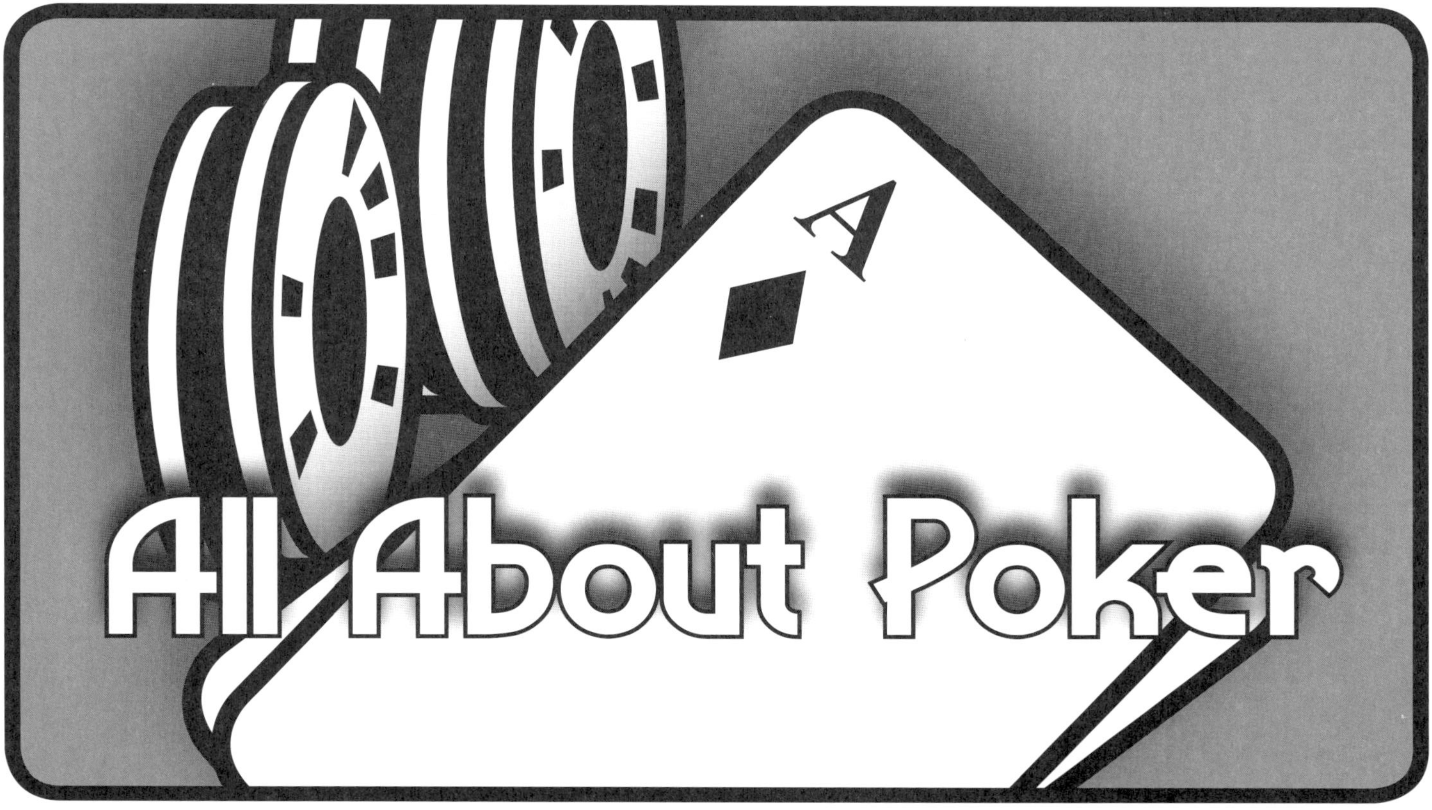

All About Poker
A

A ♣ Poker History

Though many have tried, finding the true origin of the game of poker has proven to be a daunting task. There are several theories on how and where poker began, though none that can be confirmed. It is pretty apparent, however, that poker is a game that was not born or created, but rather, a game that has evolved. Here are some of the speculations of how poker may have come to be the popular card game as the world now knows of it.

China 900 BC

One theory is that poker evolved from a game that the Chinese Emperor, Mu-tsung, played in 969 BC. The story explains that poker may have derived from Chinese dominoes and evolved from the game of "domino cards" the Emperor and his wife played on New Year's Eve.

Germany 13ᵗʰ Century

Some historians say poker evolved from the German game of pochspeil. The game involved bluffing and players would indicate whether they wanted to pass or open by knocking on the table and saying, "Ich Poche!"

New Orleans 15ᵗʰ Century

Some believe poker was created by the French who settled in New Orleans around 1480. The game was called "poque" and involved bluffing and betting. This is also believed to be the first instance of using a deck consisting of clubs, diamonds, hearts and spades.

Persia 16ᵗʰ Century

Another theory states that poker may have originated from the Persian game "as nas". This 5-player game required a special deck of 25 cards with 5 suits.

A♣ Poker History

Mississippi River 19th Century

In his writing, Jonathon H. Green makes one of the earliest known written references to poker. He wrote of the "cheating game", which was being played on the Mississippi riverboats. Green chose to call the game Poker, after not being able to find other references to the game. He described a 2 to 4-player game using only the aces, kings, queens, jacks and tens. From the riverboats, poker soon spread by way of wagon and train. During the Civil War, modifications of the game, such as stud poker, the draw and the straight became popular. The joker was introduced as a wild card in 1875.

America, 20th Century

In 1910, Nevada passed a law making it illegal to run a betting game. However, the game of poker was declared a game of skill by the Attorney General of California. Therefore, antigambling laws could not stop people from playing the game. Stud poker was declared illegal, as it was a game based solely on chance. Because of this, draw poker games developed and gained popularity. In 1931, Nevada reversed its decision to legalize casino gambling.

Today

Poker has evolved, through many backroom games, riverboats and saloons, into the present day game that is played in homes and casinos everywhere. Though poker is now regulated by gambling laws, it still remains the most popular card game in the world. The game has grown into a sporting event, with competitions and tournaments taking place daily. The pinnacle of all poker events, The World Series of Poker, attracts players from all over the globe, competing for money and the chance to wear the title of the world's top poker players.

The Rules

While there are many different forms of poker, these are the basic rules to regular poker, also known as 5-card draw or draw poker. Poker is played with a standard 52 card deck (without jokers) with four suits of equal value; clubs, diamonds, hearts and spades. The cards within each suit rank in the following order (from highest to lowest):

Ace
King
Queen
Jack
10
9
8
7
6
5
4
3
2

The dealer will deal 5 cards, one at a time, to each player. From those 5 cards, each player tries to play the highest hand of the game and, therefore, would be the winner. The players take turns betting on their hand. This is where the element of "bluffing" enters the game. The players may try to fool each other by staying in the game to make the other players think that he or she has a winning hand. The fun of the game is never knowing what the other players are holding, and trying to fool each other into thinking your hand is better or worse than it actually is.

Card Combinations

The various hands that a player can have are listed here in order of rank:

Card	Explanation
Royal Flush 10 J Q K A	This is the most valuable poker hand and beats all other poker hands. The hand consists of a 10, J, Q, K and A all of the same suit.
Straight Flush 2 3 4 5 6 9 10 J Q K	This hand beats all hands except for the Royal Flush. To achieve a straight flush, the hand would consist of five cards of the same suit in numerical order. For example, 2, 3, 4, 5 and 6 of the same suit. If there are two Straight Flushes in the game, the flush with the highest card values would win. A 9, 10, J, Q, K flush would beat the lower flush listed previously. A Straight Flush is not allowed to "wrap around". For example, Q, K, A, 2, 3 is worth nothing.
Four of a Kind 5 5 5 5 J	Four cards of the same numerical value. For example, a hand of 5, 5, 5, 5, J would be a Four of a Kind. If there are two hands of this rank at the table, the Four of a Kind with a greater face value would win.
Full House J J J 4 4 K K K 3 3	This is a hand where 3 out of the 5 cards have the same face value and the remaining 2 cards have the same face value. For example, a hand of J, J, J, 4, 4. A tie would be broken by the hand with the higher values winning. If a tie still remains, the winner would be determined by the higher of the three matching cards. For example, K, K, K, 3, 3 would beat Q, Q, Q, A, A.
Flush 2 4 7 J K	All five cards of the same suit, in any order. For example, 2, 4, 7, J and K of hearts. A tie is won simply by whoever holds the highest ranking card.
Straight 3 4 5 6 7	Five cards of any suit that are in numerical order. For example, 3, 4, 5, 6, 7 of different suits. Just as in a Straight Flush, the cards cannot "wrap around." A tie is won simply by whoever holds the highest ranking card.
Three of a Kind 10 10 10 3 Q	Three cards in a hand of the same numerical rank. For example, 10, 10, 10, 3, Q. If there are multiple Three of a Kinds at the table, the winner would be determined by the higher of the three matching cards.
Two Pair 3 3 Q Q J	A hand that has two separate pairs of matching cards. For example, 3, 3, Q, Q, J. In a tie, the hand with the highest ranking pair would win.
Pair 7 7 8 10 J	A hand of one matching pair of cards. For example, 7, 7, 8, 10, J. In a tie, the hand with the highest ranking pair would win.
High Card 7 3 2 Q A	When none of the players hold any of the hands listed above, the winner is determined simply by who holds the highest value card. Ace is always the highest, with 2 being the lowest card available.

A ♣ Starting the Game

To start the game, designate one player to be the dealer. When playing at home, the dealer can also participate in the hand by dealing cards to himself or herself, as well. The dealer begins by dealing one card at a time, face-down, to each player, beginning with the player directly to his or her left. The dealer continues handing out one card at a time moving clockwise around the table. If participating in the game, the dealer deals to himself or herself last. The dealer continues handing out cards in this fashion until all players have 5 cards face-down in front of them. The remaining un-dealt cards are placed in a face-down stack in the middle of the table. The players can then pick up their 5 cards and look at them, being careful not to let other players see the values of their cards.

Token Bet

To enter the game, all players must offer an "ante" or a token bet. The amount of the "ante" is decided before the game begins. All players must place their ante in the middle of the table before looking at their cards. The money or chips gathering in the center of the table is called the "pot". By having all players offer an ante in order to play the game, it is ensured that someone will always win something on each hand.

Folding

The players look at their hand and decide if they want to stay in the game. If a player thinks he or she has a low chance of winning the hand, or does not want to risk with bluffing to the other players, he or she can fold. By folding, the player lays his or her cards, face-down in front of them and is out of the game for this hand.

A ♣ Betting

The players all have a chance to bet on their hand. Starting with the player to the direct left of the dealer, the players take turns either betting or folding for their turn. The first player can bet any amount up to the limit (which is decided before the game begins.) If the first player decides to fold, play goes to the next player clockwise who then has the chance to bet or fold. Once the first bet is placed, the remaining players can either fold, see or raise the bet. By seeing the bet, a player would match the same amount as the first bet. By raising the bet, a player would first match the bet and then raise the bet by any amount, up to the limit. If a player raises the bet, all previous players who have not folded must raise the same amount to stay in the game, or fold and be out of the hand. Once the first round is completed, all players remaining in the game can choose to get rid of 0, 1, 2, or 3 cards and replace them with cards from the face-down deck in the middle of the table to try to increase the value of their hand. It is the dealer's duty to collect and deal these new cards to the players. The old cards are discarded face-down and set aside until a new hand begins.

After the players have their new hand, they now have another chance to bet or fold, beginning with the first player to the left of the dealer who is still in the game. This round continues until there are no more raises. Everyone who matched the last bet remains in the game. All players must reveal their hand to the other players by laying their cards face-up in front of them. The player with the highest hand is the winner and collects all money from the pot. If all but one player decide to fold, the last player remaining in the game wins by default and collects all money from the pot.

The cards are then shuffled. The player to the direct left of the dealer becomes the new dealer and the game repeats, with all players placing their ante in the middle of the table before looking at their hand.

A ♣

All Chips In

When hosting a poker party at home, it is important to remember that playing poker for money is illegal in some states. Make sure you have plenty of chips for each player to bet with. About 40 chips per person is a good bet (no pun intended).

Poker Etiquette

Follow these simple etiquette tips to ensure your next poker party is a success and enjoyed by all!

•Do not act out of turn. Wait for your turn to fold or bet.

•Don't throw your chips into the pot because of the chance they might go flying the wrong way. Instead, simply slide, drop or place your chips in the pot.

•Place the proper betting amount in the pot all at once. Avoid adding one chip from your stack at a time.

•To keep the play moving, make decisions in a timely manner.

•After viewing your cards, keep them face-down on the table in front of you.

•When it is time to reveal the hands, turn over all your cards.

•Don't discuss your hand during the game.

•If you run out of chips halfway through a hand, you must put all your chips in to stay in the game. Never bring in chips from elsewhere to add to the pot.

The Odds

This table shows the chances that a specific hand will appear in poker. The more rare the combination of cards, the more valuable the hand will be. The chance that you will receive these hands in a deal of 5 cards is...

Royal Flush	1 in 649,740
Straight Flush	1 in 64,974
Four of a Kind	1 in 4,165
Full House	1 in 694
Flush	1 in 509
Straight	1 in 255
Three of a Kind	1 in 47
Two Pair	1 in 21
One Pair	1 in 2 1/2
No Pair	1 in 2

Below is a table showing the number of possible ways to achieve a certain hand in a 52 card deck:

Straight Flush	40
Four of a Kind	624
Full House	3,744
Flush	5,108
Straight	10,200
Three of a Kind	54,912
Two Pair	123,552
One Pair	1,980,240
No Pair	1,302,540
Total Possible Hands	2,598,960

A♣ Top 10 Poker Tips

1. Most beginner players play too many of their starting hands. Instead of keeping the hand and hoping to improve your odds when cards are traded in, choose to **fold a bad starting hand**. Most top players only play between 20 and 30% of their starting hands. This will help remove some of the element of luck by beginning with a better hand.

2. **Know when to fold' em.** Many beginners will stay in the game and keep betting, regardless of what their opponent's actions are suggesting. Top players often believe it is the hands you can lay down that are the key to winning in the end.

3. If you want to win, **choose less skillful opponents** to play against. While this sounds fairly obvious, it is often a smart move to play at betting limits where you can beat the majority of the players.

4. **Watch your opponent's habits and actions closely.** The best time to observe other players is after you've folded on a hand because you are not emotionally invested in the round. Pay attention to how your opponents bet, how much they bet and what position they are in when they bet.

5. Bet on hands to gain knowledge. Betting doesn't always have to take place because you have a good hand. Many players **use betting as a way to gain information** about other player's strategy and habits. For example, re-raising could be used to check the credibility of your opponent's hand.

6. **Put yourself in your opponent's shoes.** Once you have observed your opponent's habits and gain knowledge after betting on a hand, ask yourself questions about your opponent's actions. Questions such as, "Why did he re-raise me that amount?" or "Why did he call instead of raise in the previous round?"

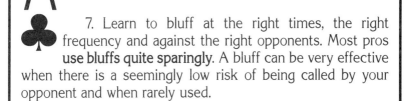

A
♣

7. Learn to bluff at the right times, the right frequency and against the right opponents. Most pros **use bluffs quite sparingly**. A bluff can be very effective when there is a seemingly low risk of being called by your opponent and when rarely used.

8. **Try to be unpredictable.** The easiest players to figure out are the tighter players who only bet when they have a good hand. Change up your style and let your opponents see that you can bluff and play some hands that start at lower values. These changes to your game should be subtle.

9. **Understand player positions.** It is important to play strong hands, as well as being in good position when you play them. The ideal betting position is the dealer, as you have the advantage of watching all the betting action that has taken place before your turn. If a lot of betting action takes place before you and you have a mediocre or low hand, it would probably be a wise decision to fold.

10. **Take notes.** Good poker players can always learn more about the game by keeping track of what works and doesn't work for them. You can learn a lot about your style of play and improve your game.

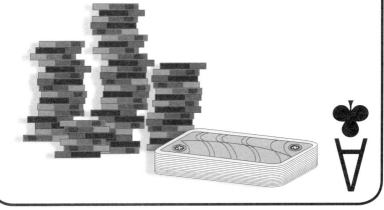

Slang, Jargon and Lingo

Before sitting down to play a hand, it would be a good idea to familiarize yourself with common poker terms.

All in: betting everything you have in front of you.

Alligator blood: a compliment given to an outstanding player who has proven their skills under great pressure.

Ante: a small forced bet that everyone at the table is required to pay before each hand.

Bad beat: when a player with a weaker hand hits a lucky card to beat a far superior hand.

Bankroll: the money a player uses to play poker with.

Base deal: cheating by dealing from the bottom of the deck.

Big slick: any ace-king combination of pocket cards.

Blind bet: a bet that is forced and must be posted before you look at any cards.

Bluff: making opponents think you have a good hand by betting or raising when you actually hold a very bad hand.

Bullets: a pair of aces in the hole.

Bump: to raise.

Bust: to run out of money, especially in a tournament.

Button: a white acrylic disk set in front of a player, used to indicate the dealer. Also used to refer to the player on the button. For example, "The button raised."

Buy: to make a bet large enough that other players are unlikely to call.

Call: to match the current bet.

Case money: emergency money.

Catch: a player is said to be catching cards when the cards are treating him or her well.

Check-raise: when a player checks and then raises after another player bets in later position.

Checks: poker chips.

Coffeehouse: to talk about a hand one is involved in, usually with the intent of misleading or manipulating other players.

Cowboys: kings.

Cut: the act of splitting the deck in half after the cards have been shuffled. The bottom half is then stacked over the top half.

Draw: to play a hand that is not yet good, but could become so if the right cards are dealt.

Drop: to fold or lose a particular amount of money.

Fish: a bad poker player who throws his or her money away at the tables.

Fold: to abandon your hand, usually because someone else has made a larger bet that you are unwilling to call.

Four flush: a hand with four cards of the same suit.

Grinder: an un-ambitious player who only hopes to win a little money on each game.

Slang, Jargon and Lingo

Heads up: a play between only two players.

Ladies: queens.

Limp in: to enter a round by calling a bet, rather than raising.

Lock: a hand that is guaranteed to win at least part of the pot.

Maniac: a player who plays extremely loose and aggressive, often raising with any hand.

Mechanic: a cheater who manipulates the cards to his or her benefit when dealing.

Monster: a hand that is almost certain to win.

Muck: the pile of folded and discarded cards in front of the dealer.

Nuts: the top hand.

Outs: live cards remaining in the deck that could improve a hand.

Paint: a card with a face on it, such as Jacks, Queens and Kings.

Pasadena: to fold.

Rabbits: a weak player. Also called a george.

Rag: a card, usually a low card, which has no apparent impact on a hand.

Rainbow: three or four cards of different suits.

Raise: to increase the amount of the bet after someone has opened betting in a round.

Rake: the percentage of the pot that the house keeps.

River: the final card dealt in a poker hand.

Rock garden: a game of extremely tight players.

Round: can refer to either a round of betting or a round of hands.

Rounder: an experienced player who earns his or her living at the poker tables.

Seconds: a style of cheating, in which the dealer gives out the second card from the top of the deck, keeping the top card for themselves.

Speed: the level of aggressiveness with which a player conducts their hands.

Snap off: to beat a player, often a bluffer, with a hand that is not especially great.

Spikes: a pair of aces.

Tap: to bet the amount of an opponent's entire stack, forcing him or her to go "all in" if they call the bet.

Tapioca: out of money.

Tell: an unconscious gesture that reveals information about a player's hand.

Toke: a small amount of money given to the dealer by the winner of a pot.

Under the gun: the first player to bet.

Underdog: the player who is unlikely to win when two hands face off.

Poker Face

A ♣

You can learn a lot by watching the face and expressions of your opponents. Often, a player will subconsciously react, revealing very important information about their hand. Watch for these behaviors...

The Eyes

Many pro players wear sunglasses or visors when playing because they know that the eyes rarely lie. For example, many players can't help but stare at cards they wish to rid. Also, if a player is looking to steal the pot, he or she may look quickly to their left to see if the remaining players, you have yet to act, are likely to fold. Players may also try to ask questions about your hand, knowing that someone can rarely look you straight in the eyes while being dishonest.

The Face

Pros try to stare down their opponents by studying their faces for nervousness or repetitive characteristics like a "twitch". Players may show obvious unhappiness in their faces when holding a weak hand, or a contrasting confidence when holding a strong hand.

The Composure

Many players like to be actors, trying to pretend as if they are disinterested when holding a great hand. Also, some players may increase the level of his or her voice while raising the pot to run a bluff.

Anxiety

It has been proven that physical changes occur in the body when confronted or faced with adversity. Actions such as flexing of muscles, eye pupil dilation, dry throat or palpitating heart rate are signs of anxiety. When a player has a good hand, they are typically ready for confrontation and can exhibit some of these characteristics. Look for things like shaking hands, the chest expanding abnormally, changes in posture or continuous peeking at their cards.

♣ **A**

A
♦

There are many variations to the game of poker. The rules of standard poker, also known as draw poker, or 5-card draw, are explained on page 4-7. Here are the basic rules of some other popular poker games.

Texas Hold'Em

Texas Hold'Em is the most popular version of poker played in the U.S. To play, two cards are dealt face down to each player and five community cards are dealt face up in the center of the table. Each player tries to make their best possible hand from any combination of the five cards in the center of the table (community cards) and the two cards (pocket cards) in his or her hand. The scoring hands are the same as in draw poker, which are explained on page 5.

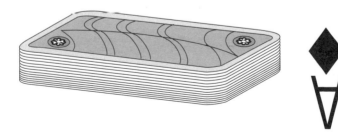

Omaha

Omaha is a variation of Texas Hold'Em, however, players are each dealt four cards. Just as in Texas Hold'Em, five community cards are dealt face up in the center of the table. The players try to create the best combination from these cards. The trick is that the combination must be made up of only two pocket cards and three of the community cards. The scoring hands are the same as in draw poker, which are explained on page 5.

Crazy Pineapple

This game is essentially the same as Texas Hold'Em, though the players are dealt three pocket cards instead of two. After the first betting round, each player must discard one of their pocket cards to the dealer. The scoring hands are the same as in draw poker, which are explained on page 5.

Seven Card Stud

To begin, each player is dealt two cards face down on the table in front of them and a third card is placed face-up. The players take a round of betting. Another card is placed face-up in front of each player and another betting round takes place. This pattern continues by placing a 5th face-up card, betting, then a 6th face-up card and betting. Finally, the seventh card is dealt face-down to each player and a final bet takes place. When all betting has finished, all cards are revealed and each player makes their best possible combination out of the seven cards dealt to them. The scoring hands are the same as in draw poker, which are explained on page 5.

Razz

Razz is the same game as Seven Card Stud, but with a twist. The player with the lowest hand in the end wins the pot. Straights and flushes are not counted, so the highest possible hand that could be achieved is 5-4-3-2-A, though the lowest hand is desired to win the game.

Guts Poker

To begin, all players pay an ante and five cards are dealt to each player. The players begin each round by deciding to play or fold. The players who stay in the round place their bets. The players continue playing and betting until one player wins the game. Any other players who remain in the game until the end, though they lose, have to either match the amount in the pot or pay another ante. The scoring hands are the same as in draw poker, which are explained on page 5.

All For One

Five cards are dealt to each player. The players follow one round of betting. Then each player, beginning with the player directly to the left of the dealer, has a chance to trade in either 1 or all 5 cards. A second round of betting takes place and then the cards are revealed. The scoring hands are the same as in draw poker, which are explained on page 5.

Dr. Pepper

This game begins the same as basic draw poker. However, 2s, 4s and 10s are wild cards and can be used to represent any card for that player. The scoring hands are the same as in draw poker, which are explained on page 5.

Frustration

This is a game of two card draw poker. Each player is dealt two cards. A round of betting takes place and players can trade in one card, if desired. Another round of betting takes place before the cards are revealed. The only winning combination would be a pair. If no one holds a pair, the winner is determined by the player holding the high card. If more than one player holds the same high card, the winner is determined by the highest second card between those players.

Heinz

This game begins the same as basic draw poker. However, 5s and 7s are wild cards and can be used to represent any card for that player. The scoring hands are the same as in draw poker, which are explained on page 5.

Italian Poker

Five cards are dealt to each player. One round of betting takes place and then the dealer places 2 cards face-up in the center of the table. The dealer places a coin or a chip to indicate the first card flipped over. Each player, beginning with the player directly to the left of the dealer, has a chance to trade in 1 or 2 cards. If a player chooses to trade in 2 cards, they are given the 2 face-up cards from the table. If a player chooses to trade in only 1 card, they are given the first face-up card from the center of the table (which is indicated by the coin or chip). When cards are taken from the center of the table, the cards are replaced with either 1 or 2 face-up cards and the next player has the choice to trade in cards. Another round of betting takes place and the cards are revealed. The scoring hands are the same as in draw poker, which are explained on page 5.

A

◆ Kings & Little Ones

This game begins the same as basic draw poker. However, Kings and the lowest card in each player's hand are wild cards and can be used to represent any card for that player. A hand of 5-J-Q-Q-K would be played as 4 Queens (Four of a Kind), because the King is wild and so is the 5, since it is the lowest card in the hand. Aces can be played as either the high or low card, at each player's discretion. The scoring hands are the same as in draw poker, which are explained on page 5.

Straight No Draw

This is probably the simplest version of poker. Five cards are dealt to each player. Each player tries to make the best possible hand from the cards they've been dealt. No cards are wild and no cards can be traded in. One betting round takes place and the cards are revealed. Bluffing is a major element to this game. The scoring hands are the same as in draw poker, which are explained on page 5.

A
◆ Three Legged Race

Each player tries to win "legs" by having either the best or lowest hand of each round. After each round, one "leg" is awarded to the player with the highest hand and the player with the lowest hand. The first player to have three "legs" wins the pot. The scoring hands are the same as in draw poker, which are explained on page 5. The lowest hand would be determined by the player holding the "worst" cards, according to the draw poker hands on page 5.

Trees

Five cards are dealt to each player. One betting round takes place. The players are allowed to freely exchange cards, receiving the same number of cards as given away. When all players have finished trading, another betting round takes place and the cards are revealed. The scoring hands are the same as in draw poker, which are explained on page 5.

If you are new to the game and like to keep things simple, throwing an Amateur Night party would be a great bet. Mix up simple, non-alcoholic cocktails and prepare easy, yet delicious snacks for all your friends!

Amateur Night

Roy Rogers (Cherry Coke)

Makes 2 servings

Ice cubes
Dash of grenadine syrup
Cola

2 maraschino cherries
2 orange slices

Fill two tall glasses with ice. Add a dash of grenadine syrup to each serving and fill glasses with cola. Garnish each serving with a maraschino cherry and an orange slice.

Shirley Temple

Makes 2 servings

Ice cubes
2 oz. grenadine syrup
16 oz. club soda or 7-up

2 maraschino cherries
2 orange slices

Fill two tall glasses with ice. Add a dash of grenadine syrup to each serving and fill glasses with club soda or 7-up. Garnish each serving with a maraschino cherry and an orange slice.

A ♠

Herbed Cheese Cracker Bites

Makes 18 to 20 servings

2 (10 1/2 oz.) boxes
   cheese crackers
1/2 C. vegetable oil
1 (1 oz.) env. ranch
   dressing mix

1 T. dried dillweed
1 tsp. garlic powder
1 tsp. celery salt

In a large ziplock bag, place cheese crackers. In a medium bowl, combine vegetable oil, ranch dressing mix, dried dillweed, garlic powder and celery salt. Mix until well combined and pour over crackers in bag. Close bag securely and toss until crackers are evenly coated. Place in refrigerator for 24 hours, turning back and forth occasionally. Remove from refrigerator. Let crackers warm to room temperature before serving. Store leftovers in an airtight container.

A
♠ Cheddar Poker Dip

Makes 8 to 10 servings

1 small roll Jimmy Dean
   sausage
1 (8 oz.) pkg. cream cheese,
   softened
1 (12 oz.) bottle chili sauce

1 red bell pepper, chopped
1 small onion, chopped
1 1/2 C. shredded Cheddar
   cheese

Cook sausage according to package directions. Drain and crumble cooked sausage and set aside. In a 9x13" baking dish, spread an even layer of cream cheese. Pour chili sauce over cream cheese and sprinkle crumbled sausage over cream cheese. Add chopped red bell pepper and chopped onion in a single layer over sausage. Sprinkle shredded Cheddar cheese over mixture. Serve with various chips and crackers for dipping.

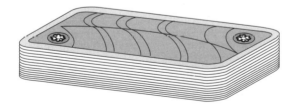

Pacific Sunset Cocktails

Makes 2 servings

Ice cubes
1 1/2 C. pineapple juice, chilled

2/3 C. orange juice, chilled
2 T. grenadine syrup
Lime wedges for garnish

Into two tall glasses filled with ice, slowly pour 3/4 cup pineapple juice into each serving. Add 1/3 cup orange juice to each glass and add grenadine syrup. Do not stir, as the juices will take on the look of a sunset. Garnish each serving with a lime wedge.

Cherry Limeade

Makes 2 servings

Ice cubes
Juice of 2 large limes
4 T. cherry syrup

Lemon lime soda
2 maraschino cherries

Fill two tall glasses with ice. Add half of the lime juice and 2 tablespoons cherry syrup to each glass. Fill glasses with lemon lime soda. Garnish each serving with a maraschino cherry.

A ♠

Wagon Wheel Cocktails

Makes 2 servings

2/3 C. orange juice, chilled
2/3 C. apple cider, chilled
2 oz. vodka

2 thick orange slices
2 toothpicks
4 maraschino cherries

In a cocktail shaker filled with ice, combine orange juice, apple cider and vodka. Shake well and divide into two highball glasses filled with ice. To prepare a wagon wheel, slide a thick orange slice onto a toothpick. Anchor both sides of the orange slice with one maraschino cherry. Garnish drink with wagon wheel. Repeat with other orange slice and cherries for the remaining drink.

Strawberry Daiquir-tease

Makes 2 servings

3/4 C. frozen strawberries
    in syrup
2 oz. fresh lime juice
2 tsp. sugar

Ice cubes
2 whole strawberries
2 orange slices

In a cocktail shaker filled with ice, combine strawberries in syrup, lime juice and sugar. Shake vigorously and strain into tall glasses filled with crushed ice. Garnish each serving with a whole strawberry and an orange slice.

Easy Spiced Nuts

Makes 3 cups

1 egg white
1 T. water
3 C. assorted nuts, such as
  macadamia nuts, pecans,
  almonds or walnuts

1/4 C. sugar
1/2 tsp. salt
1 tsp. cinnamon
1/4 tsp. ground cloves
1/4 tsp. nutmeg

Preheat oven to 300°. In a large bowl, beat egg white and water until mixture is foamy. Add assorted nuts and toss until evenly coated. In a medium bowl, combine sugar, salt, cinnamon, ground cloves and nutmeg and sprinkle over nuts, mixing until well coated. On a lightly greased jellyroll pan, spread nuts in an even layer. Bake in oven for 25 to 30 minutes, stirring after every 10 minutes.

A
♠

Simple Shrimp
Poppers

Makes 8 to 10 servings

1 (16 oz.) tube refrigerated
   flaky dinner rolls
2 (4 1/4 oz.) can tiny
   shrimp, drained

2 T. mayonnaise
1/2 C. grated Parmesan
   cheese
1 tsp. dried oregano

Preheat broiler. Divide dinner roll dough into individual rolls. In a medium bowl, combine drained tiny shrimp, mayonnaise, grated Parmesan cheese and dried oregano. Mix until well blended. Divide mixture evenly over dinner rolls and place on a baking sheet. Place under broiler for 1 to 2 minutes, until heated throughout. Let cool for 1 minute before serving.

A ♠

Taco Snack Mix

Makes 12 cups

4 C. assorted Chex cereals
4 C. small pretzel sticks
4 C. tortilla chips

1 (1 1/2 oz.) pkg. taco
   seasoning
1/4 C. margarine, melted

In a large bowl, combine assorted Chex cereals, pretzel sticks, tortilla chips and taco seasoning. Toss until evenly incorporated. Drizzle melted butter over mixture and toss until evenly coated. Store mixture in an airtight container until ready to serve.

Grape Swizzle Punch

Makes 28 servings

2 (6 oz.) can frozen white
   grape juice concentrate
1 (46 oz.) can pineapple juice

2 (12 oz.) can lemon lime
   soda, chilled
Green grapes for garnish

In a large pitcher, prepare white grape juice according to package directions. In a large punch bowl, combine white grape juice, pineapple juice and lemon lime soda. Mix until well blended. Float green grapes in punch bowl for garnish. To serve, ladle mixture into punch glasses and garnish each serving with a few grapes.

A
Virgin Bloody Mary

Makes 10 servings

1 (46 oz.) can tomato juice
2 tsp. salt
2 tsp. ground cumin
Juice of 6 limes

8 dashes Tabasco sauce
Ice cubes
Fresh lime slices

In a large bowl, combine tomato juice, salt, ground cumin, fresh lime juice and Tabasco sauce. Mix until well blended. Transfer mixture to a pitcher. Pour mixture into highball glasses filled with ice. Garnish each serving with a lime slice.

Peaches n' Cream Colada

Makes 4 servings

4 fresh peaches	2 tsp. rum extract
1 C. pineapple juice	15 ice cubes
1/2 C. cream of coconut	

Cut peaches into slices and set aside 4 of the slices. In a blender, blend remaining peach slices until smooth. Add pineapple juice, cream of coconut, rum extract and ice cubes. Process on high until well blended and pour mixture evenly into 4 glasses. Garnish each serving with 1 peach slice.

Mock Margaritas

Makes 6 servings

1 (6 oz.) can frozen lemonade concentrate, partially thawed	1/2 C. powdered sugar
	Ice cubes
	Club soda
1 (6 oz.) can frozen limeade concentrate, partially thawed	Salt

In a blender, combine lemonade concentrate, limeade concentrate and powdered sugar. Blend until mixture is smooth. Add ice cubes and blend until frothy. Add enough club soda until margaritas are cut to desired tartness. Dip the rims of 6 margarita glasses in salt and pour blended mixture evenly into each glass.

A

♠ Guava Party Punch

Makes 50 servings

3 qts. guava or passion
    fruit juice
3 qts. cranberry juice
    cocktail

2 liters grapefruit juice
3 liters ginger ale
24 ice cubes
4 limes, halved and sliced

In a large punch bowl, combine guava fruit juice, cranberry juice cocktail, grapefruit juice and ginger ale. Add ice cubes and lime slices and stir until well blended. To serve, ladle mixture into punch glasses, garnishing each serving with a lime slice.

Thirst Quencher Punch

Makes 24 servings

2 qts. apple cider, chilled
1 (6 oz.) can frozen
    lemonade concentrate,
    thawed

1 (28 oz.) bottle ginger ale,
    chilled
Ice cubes
2 apples, sliced

In a large punch bowl, combine chilled apple cider and thawed lemonade concentrate. Add ginger ale and ice cubes and stir until well blended. Add fresh cut apple slices. To serve, ladle mixture into punch glasses, garnishing each serving with an apple slice.

A
♠

Ranch Party Mix

Makes about 18 cups

1 (1 oz.) env. ranch dressing mix
2 T. dried dillweed
6 C. assorted Chex cereals
1 (10 oz.) pkg. oyster crackers

1 C. pretzel sticks, broken into 2" pieces
1 C. bagel chips, broken
1/2 C. vegetable oil
1/4 C. butter, melted

In a large bowl, combine ranch dressing mix, dried dillweed, assorted Chex cereals, oyster crackers, broken pretzel sticks and broken bagel chips. Toss until well incorporated. In a medium bowl, combine vegetable oil and melted butter. Drizzle butter mixture over ingredients in bowl and toss until evenly coated. Transfer mixture to a large paper bag and let stand for 2 hours, shaking gently every 30 minutes. Store mixture in an airtight container.

Fuzzless Navel

Makes 2 servings

4 oz. peach nectar   12 oz. orange juice

Into two tall glasses filled with ice, pour 2 ounces peach nectar in each glass. Add 6 ounces orange juice to each glass and mix lightly. If desired, peach Schnapps can be substituted for the peach nectar to make an alcoholic version of the drink.

Sweet Amaretto Cocktails

Makes 2 servings

5 oz. amaretto   8 oz. 7-up soda
4 oz. cherry syrup   Ice cubes
8 oz. orange juice

In a blender, combine amaretto, cherry syrup, orange juice and 7-up soda. Pulse for 10 to 15 seconds until well incorporated. Add ice cubes and process on high until well blended and smooth. Pour mixture evenly into two cocktail glasses.

A ♠ Pigs in a Blanket

Makes 24 servings

2 1/4 C. flour
1 tsp. salt
3/4 C. shortening

Ice water
24 cocktail sausages

Preheat oven to 400°. Into a medium bowl, sift flour and salt. Using a pastry blender, cut in shortening. Mix in enough ice water until dough holds together. Chill dough in refrigerator. Roll out dough to 1/8" thickness. Cut dough into squares large enough to cover 1 cocktail sausage. Place 1 cocktail sausage on each dough square and wrap sides of dough up and over sausages, pinching edges to secure. Place wrapped sausages on a lightly greased baking sheet and bake in oven for 15 to 20 minutes, until pastry is lightly browned. Remove from oven and serve immediately.

Chocolate Dream

Makes 2 servings

2 oz. banana flavored liqueur   8 oz. chocolate milk
4 oz. crème de cacao   Whipped topping
4 scoops chocolate ice cream   2 maraschino cherries
2 oz. chocolate syrup

    In a blender, combine banana flavored liqueur, crème de cacao, chocolate ice cream, chocolate syrup and chocolate milk. Process on high until well blended and smooth. Pour mixture evenly into two parfait glasses. Top each serving with a dollop of whipped topping and 1 maraschino cherry.

Cranberry Spritzers

Makes 2 servings

1 oz. amaretto   Twist of lime for garnish
1/2 C. cranberry juice   1 oz. lemon lime soda
1 C. club soda

    Into two chilled highball glasses filled with ice, add 1/2 ounce amaretto, 1/4 cup cranberry juice and 1/2 cup club soda to each glass. Mix lightly and garnish each serving with a twist of lime. Pour 1/2 ounce lemon lime soda into each glass and serve.

A
♠

Salsa Bites

Makes 24 servings

2 (one 8 oz., one 3 oz.) pkgs. cream cheese, softened
1/3 C. thick n' chunky salsa
2 eggs
1/2 C. shredded Cheddar cheese

2 T. chopped pitted olives
1 T. chopped green onion
1 clove garlic, pressed
1/4 C. sour cream
2 T. fresh chopped cilantro

Preheat oven to 350°. In a medium bowl, beat cream cheese until smooth. Add salsa and eggs and mix until well blended. Add shredded Cheddar cheese, chopped olives, chopped green onion and pressed garlic. Mix well. Generously grease 24 mini muffin cups. Spoon about 1 tablespoon of the mixture into each muffin cup. Bake in oven for 15 to 18 minutes, until center of salsa bites are set. Remove from oven and let cool in pan for 5 minutes. Remove from muffin cups and let cool completely on a wire rack. In a separate bowl, combine sour cream and fresh chopped cilantro. Mix well. Serve mixture with salsa bites for dipping.

A ♠ Sweet & Sour Won Tons

Makes 54 servings

1 lb. ground pork
1/2 C. chopped water
   chestnuts
Pinch of salt

1 T. soy sauce
1 egg, beaten
2 green onions, chopped
1 pkg. won ton wrappers

In a medium bowl, combine ground pork, chopped water chestnuts, salt, soy sauce, beaten egg and chopped green onions. Mix well and place one teaspoon of the mixture on each won ton wrapper. Fold wrappers according to package directions. In a large skillet over medium high heat, place vegetable oil. Add won ton wrappers and cook, turning once, until golden on both sides. Serve warm with Sweet and Sour Sauce (recipe below).

Sweet & Sour Sauce

Makes about 1 cup

1 T. soy sauce
1/2 C. sugar
1/3 C. pineapple juice
1/4 C. ketchup

1/2 C. apple cider vinegar
2 T. cornstarch
2 T. water

In a medium bowl, combine soy sauce, sugar, pineapple juice, ketchup and apple cider vinegar. In a small bowl, combine cornstarch and water, mixing until cornstarch is completely dissolved. Add cornstarch mixture to soy sauce mixture. Stir well and heat in microwave for 3 to 5 minutes, stirring after every minute. Remove and let stand until thickened. Use as dipping sauce for Sweet & Sour Won Tons.

Hodge Podge Mix

Makes 8 to 10 servings

1/4 C. butter
1 (12 oz.) pkg. chocolate chips
1 C. creamy peanut butter
1 (12 oz.) box Golden Grahams cereal

1 C. golden raisins
3 C. roasted, salted peanuts
2 3/4 C. powdered sugar

In a large saucepan over medium high heat, combine butter, chocolate chips and peanut butter. Stir until completely melted and smooth. Remove from heat and fold in Golden Grahams cereal, golden raisins and peanuts. Mix until completely coated and transfer to a large bowl. Add powdered sugar and toss until coated. Let mixture cool before serving. Store in an airtight container.

43

A ♠ Ham 'n Cheese Balls

Makes 48 servings

1 (8 oz.) pkg. cream cheese, softened
1 C. finely chopped, cooked ham
1 tsp. prepared horseradish
1/2 tsp. dry mustard
1 tsp. hot pepper sauce
1/2 C. finely chopped nuts
48 pretzel sticks

In a medium bowl, combine softened cream cheese, chopped ham, horseradish, dry mustard and hot pepper sauce. Mix until well blended and shape mixture into about 48 (3/4") balls. In a shallow dish, place finely chopped nuts. Roll cheese balls in nuts until evenly coated. Place cheese balls on a baking sheet, cover and chill in refrigerator for 4 hours. Before serving, transfer cheese balls to a serving platter and insert one pretzel stick into each ball. Serve immediately.

Southwestern Snackers

Makes 24 servings

2 T. cornmeal
2 (10 oz.) pkgs. refrigerated
   crescent rolls
1 (14 oz.) can refried black
   beans, drained
2 tsp. chili powder

1 1/2 C. shredded Cheddar
   cheese
2 plum tomatoes, chopped
2 green onions, minced
1/2 C. chopped pitted olives
1 C. salsa, optional

Preheat oven to 350°. Sprinkle a stoneware baking dish generously with cornmeal. Unroll crescent rolls into 4 triangles and pinch sides together. Form dough into a rectangle large enough to cover 9x13" baking dish, pressing on bottom and up sides of baking dish. Bake in oven for 18 to 20 minutes, or until crust is golden brown. In a medium bowl, combine black beans and chili powder. Mix well and spread over crust. Sprinkle shredded cheese evenly over crust. Sprinkle chopped tomatoes, minced onions and chopped olives over cheese. Using a pizza cutter, cut mixture into squares. If desired, serve with salsa for dipping.

Easy Cheesy Bites

Makes 35 servings

1/2 C. butter, softened
1 C. flour
1/4 tsp. cayenne pepper

1 tsp. paprika
2 C. shredded sharp
    Cheddar cheese

Preheat oven to 190°. In a medium bowl, combine butter, flour, cayenne pepper and paprika. Mix until well blended and add shredded sharp Cheddar cheese. Stir until well combined and shape mixture into bite-size balls. Arrange cheese balls in a single layer on a baking sheet. Bake in oven for 10 minutes. Remove from oven and let cool for 1 minute before serving.

Super Rum Smoothie

Makes 2 servings

2 bananas, sliced
2 C. sliced fresh strawberries
2 C. chunked pineapple

4 C. ice cubes
2 oz. spiced rum, optional

In a blender, combine sliced bananas, sliced strawberries, chunked pineapple and ice cubes. Process on high until well blended. If desired, add rum and blend for an additional 10 to 15 seconds. If mixture is too thick, add a little water and blend until smooth. Pour mixture evenly into two tall glasses and serve immediately.

A
Grape Crush

Makes 2 servings

6 oz. grape juice
2 oz. cranberry juice

2 oz. lemon lime soda
7-up soda

In a cocktail shaker filled with ice, combine grape juice and cranberry juice. Divide mixture evenly into two tall glasses filled with ice. Add 1 ounce lemon lime soda to each serving. Fill each glass with 7-up soda and stir lightly. Serve immediately.

Candied Nuts

Makes 10 to 12 servings

3 T. butter
1/4 C. sugar

1/4 tsp. salt
1 1/2 lbs. assorted nuts

In a large skillet over medium heat, place butter. When butter is completely melted, stir in sugar and salt, mixing until sugar and salt are completely dissolved. Add assorted nuts and continue to heat, stirring occasionally, until butter foams and begins to stick to the nuts. Continue to heat for an additional 2 minutes, being careful not to burn mixture. Using a slotted spoon, transfer nuts to a sheet of waxed paper to cool. Once mixture has cooled and hardened, break into pieces and serve.

Milk Chocolate Popcorn

Makes 4 servings

12 C. popped popcorn
1 (12 oz.) jar salted peanuts
1 C. corn syrup

1/4 C. butter or margarine
2 C. milk chocolate chips

In a large roasting pan, combine popcorn and salted peanuts and set aside. In a large saucepan over medium heat, combine corn syrup, butter and milk chocolate chips. Bring mixture to a boil, stirring constantly. Pour chocolate mixture over popcorn and nuts mixture and toss until well coated. Bake in oven for 45 minutes, stirring after every 15 minutes. Remove from oven and let cool completely. Store mixture in an airtight container for up to 2 weeks.

If you want to go swanky with your next poker party, this section is for you. Serve up martinis and chic appetizers for all the High Rollers in the house!

For High Rollers Only

Absolute Martini

Makes 1 serving

2 1/2 oz. vodka
1/2 oz. triple sec
2 oz. fresh lemon juice

Dash of orange bitters
Twist of lemon for garnish,
    optional

In a cocktail shaker filled with ice, combine vodka, triple sec, fresh lemon juice and orange bitters. Shake vigorously and strain into a martini glass. If desired, garnish with a twist of lemon peel.

Grapefruit Martini

Makes 1 serving

1 oz. light rum
1/2 oz. dry vermouth
1/2 oz. vodka
1 oz. cranberry juice

Juice of 1/2 lemon
2 oz. grapefruit juice
Sugar

In a cocktail shaker filled with ice, combine light rum, dry vermouth, vodka, cranberry juice, lemon juice and grapefruit juice. Dip the rim of a martini glass in sugar. Shake ingredients in cocktail shaker vigorously and strain into rimmed martini glass.

Olive Snackers

Makes 48 servings

2 C. shredded Cheddar cheese	1/2 tsp. salt
	1/2 tsp. pepper
1/2 C. margarine, softened	48 small pimento-stuffed
1 C. flour	olives

In a medium bowl, combine shredded Cheddar cheese, softened margarine, flour, salt and pepper. Mix well until a soft dough forms. Wrap a small amount of dough around each stuffed olive. Place wrapped olives on a lightly greased baking sheet and place in freezer for about 30 minutes. Wrapped olives can be frozen for up to 3 weeks before baking. Preheat oven to 400°. Remove baking sheet from freezer and place in oven. Bake olives for 10 to 15 minutes.

Citrus Martini

Makes 1 serving

4 oz. lemon flavored vodka
1 tsp. Grand Mariner liqueur
1 tsp. fresh lime juice

Twist of orange peel for
garnish, optional

In a cocktail shaker filled with ice, combine lemon flavored vodka, Grand Marnier liqueur and fresh lime juice. Shake vigorously and strain into a martini glass. If desired, garnish with a twist of orange peel.

Emerald City Martini

Makes 1 serving

3 oz. vodka
1 oz. Chartreuse (green herbal liqueur)

In a cocktail shaker filled with ice, combine vodka and Chartreuse. Shake vigorously and strain into a chilled martini glass.

A ♥ Sun-Dried Tomato Bruschetta

Makes 32 servings

1 (6 oz.) jar sun-dried
   tomatoes in oil
1 (16 oz.) baguette,
   cut into 1/2" thick slices
1/2 C. fresh chopped
   parsley

5 oz. grated Romano
   cheese
5 oz. grated Parmesan
   cheese

Preheat broiler. Thoroughly drain sun-dried tomatoes, reserving the oil. Using a pastry brush, spread reserved oil over one side of each baguette slice. Arrange slices in a single layer, oiled side up, in a 7x11" baking dish. Place under broiler for about 1 minute, until lightly browned. Chop sun-dried tomatoes into small pieces. In a medium bowl, combine chopped sun-dried tomatoes, fresh chopped parsley and grated Romano cheese. Remove bread slices from broiler and top each slice with some of the tomato mixture. Sprinkle grated Parmesan cheese over slices and place under broiler until cheese is melted, about 1 to 2 minutes. Remove from broiler and let cool slightly before serving.

♥ Apple Pie Martini

Makes 1 serving

3 oz. vanilla flavored vodka
1/2 oz. calvados
   (apple brandy)

1/2 oz. dry vermouth
Thin apple slice for
   garnish, optional

In a cocktail shaker filled with ice, combine vanilla flavored vodka, calvados and dry vermouth. Shake vigorously and strain into a martini glass. If desired, garnish with an apple slice.

Sweet Stacked Cocktail

Makes 2 servings

5 oz. vodka
5 oz. dry vermouth
4 oz. gin
3 oz. Jack Daniel's whiskey

3 oz. Southern Comfort
1 oz. Galliano
   (Italian herbal liqueur)
1/2 oz. grenadine

In a cocktail shaker filled with ice, combine vodka, dry vermouth, gin, whiskey, Southern Comfort, Galliano and grenadine. Shake vigorously and strain evenly into two chilled martini glasses.

A ♥

Sherry Stuffed Mushrooms

Makes 24 servings

1 1/2 lbs. whole mushrooms
3/4 C. butter or margarine,
   melted
1/3 C. chopped green onion

1/3 C. sherry
1 1/4 C. seasoned
   breadcrumbs

Preheat oven to 350°. Thoroughly clean mushrooms and remove the stems. Place melted butter in a shallow dish. Dip mushroom caps in melted butter and place in a 9x13" baking dish. Mince mushroom stems. In a medium saucepan over medium high heat, combine minced mushroom stems, minced green onions and remaining melted butter. Sauté mixture until mushroom stems and green onions are tender. Remove from heat and stir in sherry and seasoned breadcrumbs. Spoon mixture evenly into mushroom caps in baking dish. Bake in oven for 10 to 15 minutes, until heated throughout. Remove from oven and let cool for 2 minutes before serving.

A ♥ Smoked Salmon Dip

Makes about 3 cups

1 (8 oz.) pkg. cream cheese, softened
3/4 C. sour cream
1 T. lemon juice
1 T. minced onion
1 tsp. prepared horseradish

1/4 tsp. salt
1 1/2 C. smoked salmon, flaked or chopped
1/2 C. chopped pecans
2 T. fresh chopped parsley

In a medium bowl, combine softened cream cheese, sour cream, lemon juice, minced onion, prepared horseradish and salt. Mix until creamy and smooth. Fold in flaked smoked salmon and mix thoroughly. Transfer mixture to a serving bowl and sprinkle chopped pecans and fresh chopped parsley over dip. Serve with various crackers for dipping.

A
♥ Amontillado Martini

Makes 1 serving

3 oz. vodka   1 oz. Amontillado sherry

In a cocktail shaker filled with ice, combine vodka and Amontillado sherry. Shake vigorously and strain into a chilled martini glass. Serve with strong, robust cheese or assorted nuts.

Blue Moon Martini

Makes 1 serving

3 oz. gin   Twist of lemon for garnish
1/2 oz. blue curacao

In a cocktail shaker filled with ice, combine vodka and blue curacao. Shake vigorously and strain into a chilled martini glass. Garnish with a twist of lemon.

A ♥ Casino Clam Dip

Makes 8 servings

4 (6 1/2 oz.) cans
   chopped clams,
   drain 2 cans
1 C. minced celery
1 small onion, chopped
1 small green pepper,
   chopped

1/2 lb. cooked,
   crumbled bacon
1/4 C. butter
Ritz crackers or small
   toasted bread slices

Preheat oven to 350°. In a medium saucepan over medium heat, place butter. When butter is melted, add minced celery, chopped onion and chopped green pepper. Sauté mixture until vegetables have softened. Mix in 2 cans of drained clams and 2 cans of clams in juice. Stir until well combined and mix in cooked, crumbled bacon. Mix well and transfer mixture to a medium baking dish. Bake in oven for 30 to 45 minutes, or until mixture is lightly browned and bubbly. Serve with Ritz crackers or toasted bread slices for dipping.

Raz-tini

Makes 1 serving

1/2 oz. raspberry
   flavored vodka
1/2 oz. cointreau
Splash of lime juice
Splash of pineapple juice

Splash of cranberry juice
Splash of champagne
3 raspberries for garnish
Fresh mint sprig for
   garnish

In a cocktail shaker filled with ice, combine raspberry flavored vodka, cointreau, lime juice, pineapple juice and cranberry juice. Shake vigorously and strain into a martini glass. Add champagne and mix lightly. Garnish with raspberries and a fresh mint sprig.

Chocolate Martini

Makes 1 serving

1 oz. vanilla flavored vodka
1 oz. white crème de cacao

Cocoa powder
1 chocolate kiss

In a cocktail shaker filled with ice, combine vanilla flavored vodka and crème de cacao. Shake vigorously. Dip the rim of a chilled martini glass in cocoa powder. Strain mixture into martini glass and garnish with a chocolate kiss.

A ♥ Sparkling Martini

Makes 1 serving

1 1/2 oz. gin   2 green olives
3/4 oz. champagne

In a cocktail shaker filled with ice, combine gin and champagne. Stir lightly, cover shaker and strain into a chilled martini glass. Do not shake. Garnish with green olives.

Butterscotch Truffle Martini

Makes 1 serving

2 oz. vodka   Dash of crème de cacao
1 oz. butterscotch Schnapps   Ice cubes

In a blender, combine vodka, butterscotch Schnapps, crème de cacao and ice cubes. Process on high until ice is well crushed. Carefully pour mixture into a chilled martini glass.

A♥ Mozzarella Sourdough Bruschetta

Makes 16 servings

1 large ripe tomato,
    seeded and finely
    chopped
2 cloves garlic, minced
1 T. olive oil
1 tsp. dried basil

1/8 tsp. salt
1/8 tsp. pepper
4 slices sourdough
    bread
4 mozzarella cheese
    singles

In a medium bowl, combine chopped tomato, minced garlic, olive oil, dried basil, salt and pepper. Mix until well incorporated. Place sourdough bread slices on a baking sheet and place under broiler for 2 to 3 minutes, until lightly toasted. Remove from oven and spoon a generous amount of the mixture onto the bread slices. Top the tomato mixture on each bread slice with 1 mozzarella cheese slice. Return to broiler for 2 to 3 minutes, until cheese begins to melt. Remove from oven and cut each bread slice into 4 squares. Place bruschetta squares on a serving platter.

A ♥ Roast Beef Bites with Horseradish Sauce

Makes 24 servings

1 C. sour cream
1/4 C. prepared
   horseradish
1 (1 lb.) loaf French bread,
   cut into 24 slices

1 lb. thinly sliced roast
   beef, cut into 2" strips
1/4 C. chopped green
   onions

Preheat broiler. Place bread slices on a baking sheet and place under broiler for 1 to 2 minutes, until lightly toasted. In a small bowl, combine sour cream and prepared horseradish. Spread 1 teaspoon of the sour cream mixture over one side of each bread slice. Top with 1 or 2 of the roast beef strips. Top with another dollop of the sour cream mixture and sprinkle chopped green onions over each serving.

Poker Martini

Makes 1 serving

1 oz. sweet vermouth
1/2 oz. light rum

Twist of lime for garnish

In a cocktail shaker filled with ice, combine sweet vermouth and light rum. Shake vigorously and strain into a chilled martini glass. Garnish with a twist of lime peel.

Dried Fruit Party Mix

Makes 8 to 10 servings

2 C. dried mangoes, coarsely chopped
1 C. dried pineapple chunks, halved
1 C. dried tart cherries
1 C. dried banana chips
1 C. chocolate covered raisins

1 C. white chocolate or yogurt covered pretzels
1/2 C. salted pistachios, shelled
1 (3 1/4 oz.) jar macadamia nuts

In a large bowl, combine dried mangoes, dried pineapple chunks, dried tart cherries, dried banana chips, chocolate covered raisins, pretzels, pistachios and macadamia nuts. Toss until well incorporated and serve.

A ♥

Shrimp Cocktail

Makes about 15 servings

1 gallon water
2 T. plus 1 tsp. salt, divided
1 lemon
1 lb. shrimp
1 pint chili sauce

2 oz. tomato juice
2 oz. prepared horseradish
1/2 tsp. white pepper
1 tsp. dry mustard
1 T. Worcestershire sauce

To prepare shrimp, in a large pot over medium high heat, combine water, 2 tablespoons salt and 1/2 of the lemon. Bring mixture to a boil and add shrimp. Cook shrimp in boiling water for 3 to 5 minutes. Remove from heat and drain shrimp through a colander. Run shrimp under cool running water and drain again. Peel and devein the shrimp. Meanwhile, to prepare sauce, in a medium bowl, combine chili sauce, tomato sauce, prepared horseradish, white pepper, remaining 1 teaspoon salt, dry mustard, juice from remaining 1/2 lemon and Worcestershire sauce. Mix until well blended. To serve, fill a large martini glass with the sauce mixture and hang cooked shrimp over the edge. Encourage guests to dip the shrimp in the sauce and enjoy.

Black Jack

Makes 1 serving

1 oz. blackberry brandy
1/2 oz. brandy

1/2 oz. Jagermeister
1 oz. heavy whipping cream

In a cocktail shaker filled with ice, combine blackberry brandy, brandy and Jagermeister. Shake vigorously and strain into a chilled martini glass. Pour heavy cream over cocktail and mix lightly.

Ginger Cosmopolitan

Makes 1 serving

3 oz. ginger flavored
   vodka
1 1/2 oz. cointreau or
   triple sec

3/4 oz. lime juice
1 1/2 oz. cranberry juice
Twist of lemon for
   garnish, optional

In a cocktail shaker filled with ice, combine ginger flavored vodka, cointreau, lime juice and cranberry juice. Shake vigorously and strain into a chilled martini glass. If desired, garnish with a twist of lemon peel.

Lobster Bacon Rolls

Makes 18 rolls

1/4 C. tomato juice
1 egg, well beaten
1 C. cooked, flaked
   lobster or crab meat
1/2 C. dry fine
   breadcrumbs
1 T. chopped parsley

1 T. lemon juice
1/4 tsp. salt
1/4 tsp. Worcestershire
   sauce
Pepper to taste
9 slices bacon,
   cut in half

In a medium bowl, combine tomato juice and beaten egg. Add flaked lobster meat, fine breadcrumbs, chopped parsley, lemon juice, salt, Worcestershire sauce and pepper. Mix well, until a soft dough forms. Roll mixture into 18 small logs, about 2" long. Wrap half a slice of bacon around each log and secure with a toothpick. Heat over a grill or in a large saucepan over medium heat for about 10 minutes, turning to evenly brown on all sides. When bacon is cooked throughout, remove and place on a serving platter.

Pesto Crostinis

Makes 16 servings

1 (1 lb.) loaf French bread,
cut into 32 (1/4" thick)
slices
3 C. fresh basil leaves
1/3 C. Italian vinaigrette
dressing

1/3 C. plus 1/4 C. grated
Parmesan cheese,
divided
1 (8 oz.) pkg. cream
cheese, softened

Preheat broiler. Place bread slices on a baking sheet and place under broiler for 1 to 2 minutes, until lightly toasted. In a blender, combine fresh basil leaves, vinaigrette dressing and 1/3 cup grated Parmesan cheese. Process on high until well blended. Spread cream cheese over one side of each toasted bread slice and spread a generous amount of the basil mixture over cream cheese on each slice. Sprinkle remaining 1/4 cup grated Parmesan cheese over slices and place on a serving platter.

Baked Clams

Makes 6 to 10 servings

24 cherrystone clams	1/2 C. butter, divided
1 clove garlic, minced	1 T. lemon juice
4 T. chopped green pepper	6 T. seasoned bread crumbs

Preheat oven to 450°. Carefully open clams and discard the top shell. Place clams face-up in a shallow baking dish. In a medium saucepan over medium heat, melt 1/4 cup butter. Add minced garlic and chopped green pepper and sauté until softened, about 2 to 3 minutes. Add remaining 1/4 cup butter, lemon juice and seasoned bread crumbs, mixing well. Place about 1 teaspoon of the mixture on top of each clam. Bake in oven for 10 minutes. To serve, arrange baked clams on a serving platter.

A ♥ Provolone Canapes

Makes 16 servings

1 (12 oz.) jar pickled
    mixed vegetables,
    drained
1/4 C. chopped pimento-
    stuffed olives
2 oz. finely chopped
    salami

1 T. minced garlic
1 T. olive oil
2 (10 oz.) tubes
    refrigerated flakey
    biscuits
1/2 C. finely shredded
    provolone cheese

Finely chop the drained mixed vegetables. In a medium bowl, combine chopped mixed vegetables, chopped olives, finely chopped salami, minced garlic and olive oil. Mix well and chill in refrigerator at least 1 hour. Bake biscuits according to package directions, remove from oven and let cool slightly. Adjust oven temperature, if needed, to 400°. Scoop out the center of the biscuits and discard. Remove mixture from refrigerator and fold in shredded provolone cheese. Fill each biscuit with about 1 tablespoon of the cheese mixture. Place on a baking sheet and bake in oven for 8 to 10 minutes, or until biscuits are heated throughout. Remove from oven and serve warm.

Dill Shrimp Dip

Makes about 3 cups

1 (4 1/4 oz.) can tiny
   shrimp, drained
2 C. mayonnaise

1/2 C. chopped black
   olives
1 T. dried dillweed

In a medium bowl, combine drained tiny shrimp, mayonnaise, chopped black olives and dried dillweed. Mix until well blended. Serve with various crackers or cut vegetables for dipping.

Buckeye Martini

Makes 1 serving

3 oz. gin
1/2 oz. dry vermouth

1 stuffed black olive
   for garnish

In a lowball glass filled with ice, place gin. Add dry vermouth and stir lightly. Strain mixture into a chilled martini glass and garnish with a stuffed black olive.

A♥ Artichoke Cheddar Snackers

Makes 20 servings

1 (1 lb.) loaf French bread,
   cut into 20 slices
1 (6 oz.) jar marinated
   artichoke hearts,
   drained and chopped
1/4 C. chopped roasted
   red peppers

2 T. chopped green onions
1 (10 oz.) pkg. extra sharp
   Cheddar cheese,
   cut into 20 slices

   Preheat broiler. Place bread slices on a baking sheet and place under broiler for 1 to 2 minutes, until lightly toasted. In a medium bowl, combine chopped artichoke hearts, chopped red peppers and chopped green onions. Divide the artichoke mixture evenly over the bread slices. Place 1 extra sharp Cheddar cheese slice over mixture on each bread slice and return to broiler for 2 to 3 minutes, until cheese begins to melt. Remove from oven and place on a serving platter.

A ♥

Spinach Poppers

Makes 6 to 8 dozen

2 (10 oz.) pkgs. frozen
   chopped spinach,
   thawed and drained
3 C. herb stuffing mix
1 large onion, finely
   chopped
6 eggs, well beaten

3/4 C. butter, melted
1/2 C. grated Parmesan
   cheese
1 T. pepper
1 1/2 tsp. garlic salt
1/2 tsp. dried thyme

Preheat oven to 325°. In a large bowl, combine thoroughly drained spinach, stuffing mix, finely chopped onion, well beaten eggs, melted butter, grated Parmesan cheese, pepper, garlic salt and dried thyme. Mix until well combined. Roll mixture into 1/2" to 3/4" balls. Place spinach balls on a lightly greased baking sheet and bake in oven for 20 to 25 minutes. Remove from oven and let drain on paper towels before serving.

If you want to get down to the nitty gritty and play some real poker, don't mess with frilly drinks and elegant appetizers. Prepare basic party foods for all your guests and shake up some cocktails with bite to 'em!

Down & Dirty Party

Kamikaze

Makes 1 serving

2 oz. vodka   1 oz. lime juice
2 oz. triple sec   Ice cubes

In a cocktail shaker filled with ice, combine vodka, triple sec and lime juice. Shake vigorously and strain into a highball glass over ice.

T-∩-T
(Tequila n' Tonic)

Makes 1 serving

Ice cubes   Tonic water
1 1/2 oz. tequila   Lime wedge for garnish

Fill a lowball glass with ice cubes. Pour tequila over ice and add tonic water to fill glass. Mix lightly and garnish with a lime wedge.

A ♣
BBQ Pulled Pork Sandwiches

Makes 12 servings

3 T. paprika
1 T. garlic powder
1 T. brown sugar
1 T. dry mustard
3 T. coarse salt

1 (5 to 7 lb.) pork roast
1 (18 oz.) bottle barbecue
   sauce, any kind
12 hamburger buns

In a small bowl, combine paprika, garlic powder, brown sugar, dry mustard and coarse salt. Mix until well combined and rub generously over pork roast. Cover and refrigerate for 1 hour or overnight. Preheat oven to 300°. Place pork roast in a roasting pan and cook in oven for about 6 hours, or until roast reaches an internal temperature of 170° F on a meat thermometer. Roast is done when it is falling from the bone. Remove pork from roasting pan and pull meat from roast and shred. Place shredded meat in a large bowl and pour desired amount of barbecue sauce over meat, tossing until well coated. To serve, spoon pulled pork mixture onto hamburger buns.

A ♣

Olive Cracker Spread

Makes 12 servings

2 (3 oz.) pkgs. cream
   cheese, softened
1 (6 oz.) can pitted black
   olives, chopped
1 (5 oz.) can pitted green
   olives, chopped

3 T. fresh chopped parsley
1/2 tsp. crushed red
   pepper flakes
Salt and pepper to taste
4 T. sesame seeds

In a medium bowl, using a wire whisk, whip cream cheese until softened. Fold in chopped black olives, chopped green olives, fresh chopped parsley and crushed red pepper flakes. Season with salt and pepper to taste. If desired, transfer mixture to a serving bowl. Sprinkle sesame seeds over mixture. Spread dip over various crackers or pieces of bread.

Cognac Highball

Makes 1 serving

Ice cubes
2 oz. cognac
Ginger ale

Twist of lemon peel
for garnish

Fill a highball glass with ice cubes. Pour cognac over ice and add ginger ale to fill glass. Mix lightly and garnish with a twist of lemon peel.

Red Hot Hurricane

Makes 1 serving

Ice cubes
1/2 oz. bourbon
1/2 oz. amaretto
1/2 oz. Southern Comfort
1/4 oz. sloe gin

Dash of triple sec
Dash of orange juice
Dash of pineapple juice
Slice of orange for garnish

Fill a hurricane glass with ice cubes. Pour bourbon, amaretto, Southern Comfort, sloe gin, triple sec, orange juice and pineapple juice over ice. Mix lightly and garnish with an orange slice.

A ♣

Star Wars

Makes 1 serving

1 oz. blended whiskey   1 tsp. powdered sugar
1 oz. gin   Ice cubes
1 T. lemon juice

In a cocktail shaker filled with ice, combine blended whiskey, gin, lemon juice and powdered sugar. Shake vigorously and strain into a highball glass over ice.

Boilermaker

Makes 1 serving

1 (12 oz.) can or bottle   1 1/2 oz. blended whiskey
   beer, any kind

Fill a mug or pilsner glass with beer. Pour blended whiskey into a shot glass. Drop shot glass into mug of beer and drink. If preferred, drink whiskey straight and follow with beer as a chaser.

Mexican Mix

Makes 15 to 20 servings

1 (10 oz.) box toasted
  oats cereal
1 (7.2 oz.) bag cheddar
  flavored fish crackers
1 (21 oz.) box cinnamon
  Life cereal
1 (15 oz.) bag pretzel
  sticks
1 (12 oz.) pkg. sesame
  sticks

2 (12 oz.) jars dry
  roasted peanuts
2 C. butter
1/2 C. vegetable oil
1/4 C. onion powder
1/4 C. garlic powder
4 tsp. chili powder
Dash of Tabasco sauce

Preheat oven to 250°. In a large roasting pan, combine toasted oats cereal, cheddar fish crackers, Life cereal, pretzel sticks, sesame sticks and dry roasted peanuts. Toss until well incorporated. In a large microwave-safe bowl, place butter. Heat in microwave, stirring occasionally, until butter is completely melted. Remove from microwave and immediately stir in vegetable oil, onion powder, garlic powder, chili powder and Tabasco sauce, stirring until well blended. Pour over ingredients in roasting pan, tossing until evenly coated. Bake in oven for 45 minutes, stirring after every 15 minutes. Store in an airtight container.

♣ Seasoned Pretzels

Makes 6 to 10 servings

1/2 C. butter, melted
2 (1 oz.) pkg. Italian
    dressing mix
1 T. dry dillweed

1 T. onion powder or
    garlic powder
2 (16 oz.) bags mini
    twist pretzels

In a medium bowl, combine melted butter, Italian dressing mix, dry dillweed and onion powder. Mix well. Place twist pretzels in a large serving bowl and pour melted butter mixture over pretzels. Toss until evenly coated. Place in refrigerator for 1 hour before serving.

The Colonel

Makes 1 serving

1 1/2 oz. bourbon
1/2 oz. benedictine

Twist of lemon for garnish

In a cocktail shaker filled with ice, combine bourbon and benedictine. Shake vigorously and strain into a highball glass over ice. Garnish with a twist of lemon.

A♣

Party Crunch

Makes 10 servings

1/4 C. butter, melted
2 T. soy sauce
1 tsp. seasoned salt
1 1/2 tsp. Worcestershire
   sauce
Dash of Tabasco sauce
1/4 tsp. garlic powder
1 C. chow mein noodles

1 C. small pretzel sticks,
   broken into
   1 1/2" pieces
1 C. rice Chex cereal
1 C. wheat Chex cereal
1/2 C. pecans
1/2 C. cashews or
   salted peanuts

Preheat oven to 250°. In a medium bowl, combine melted butter, soy sauce, seasoned salt, Worcestershire sauce, Tabasco sauce and garlic powder. Stir until well blended. In a 9x13" baking dish, combine chow mein noodles, broken pretzel sticks, rice Chex cereal, wheat Chex cereal, pecans and cashews. Toss until well coated and pour butter mixture over cereal mixture. Stir to coat evenly. Bake in oven for 1 hour, stirring after every 15 minutes. Remove from oven and serve warm or cold.

A ♣ Spicy Bean Dip

Makes 6 servings

1 small onion, chopped
1 T. butter
1/2 tsp. chili powder
1/2 tsp. ground cumin
1 (14 oz.) can borlotti
    beans, drained
    and rinsed

1/2 C. shredded sharp
    Cheddar cheese
Salt and pepper to taste

In a medium saucepan over medium high heat, sauté chopped onion in butter, until softened. Add chili powder and ground cumin and heat for another minute. In a blender or food processor, puree borlotti beans until smooth, adding a little water if necessary. Add pureed beans to saucepan and continue to heat until cooked throughout. Remove from heat and mix in shredded sharp Cheddar cheese, mixing until cheese is completely melted. Season with salt and pepper to taste. Serve with corn chips for dipping.

Chicken Nuggets with Honey Mustard Sauce

Makes 8 servings

2 C. crushed sour cream
    and chive potato chips
1 egg
2 T. milk
6 chicken breast fillets,
    cut into 1 1/2" cubes

1/3 C. butter, melted
3/4 C. mayonnaise
3 T. honey
2 T. prepared mustard
1 T. lemon juice
2 T. orange juice

Preheat oven to 350°. Spread crushed potato chips in a shallow dish. In a small bowl, whisk together egg and milk. Dip chicken breast cubes in egg mixture and then roll in crushed potato chips until well coated. Place coated chicken cubes in a 9x13" baking dish and drizzle melted butter over chicken in dish. Bake in oven for 15 to 18 minutes, until chicken pieces are cooked throughout and coating is golden brown. Meanwhile, to prepare honey mustard sauce, in a medium bowl, combine mayonnaise, honey, prepared mustard and lemon juice. Add orange juice until sauce reaches desired consistency. Cover and chill in refrigerator until ready to serve. Serve as dipping sauce for chicken nuggets.

Cajun Chicken Wings

Makes 6 servings

1 T. vegetable oil
1 tsp. crushed red peppers
2 tsp. Cajun seasoning
1 tsp. chili powder
1/2 tsp. corn flour

6 T. brown sugar
2 C. orange juice
1 1/2 C. vinegar or
   lemon juice
2 lbs. chicken wings

In a medium bowl, combine vegetable oil, crushed red pepper, Cajun seasoning, chili powder, corn flour and brown sugar. Mix well and stir in orange juice and vinegar. Mix well and set aside 1/2 cup of the sauce. Thoroughly wash chicken wings and dry. Place chicken wings in a deep dish and pour remaining sauce over wings. Cover and chill in refrigerator for 6 hours or overnight. Preheat oven to 300°. Remove from refrigerator and place coated chicken wings on a baking dish. Bake in oven for 20 to 25 minutes, basting every 5 to 10 minutes with the reserved sauce. Serve with Blue Cheese Dip or Homemade Ranch (recipes on page 85).

A♣ Blue Cheese Dip

Makes 3 cups

1 C. crumbled blue cheese
4 oz. cream cheese,
   softened
1 1/4 C. sour cream

1 T. lemon juice
Zest of 1 lemon
2 cloves garlic, minced
Salt and pepper to taste

In a medium bowl, combine crumbled blue cheese and cream cheese. Add sour cream and mix until well blended. Add lemon juice, lemon zest and minced garlic. Season with salt and pepper to taste. Stir until well blended. Use as a dip for chicken wings or various cut vegetables. Will keep for 7 to 10 days in the refrigerator.

Homemade Ranch

Makes 1 1/2 cups

1 C. mayonnaise
1/2 C. sour cream
1/2 tsp. dried chives
1/2 tsp. dried parsley
   flakes

1/2 tsp. dried dillweed
1/4 tsp. ground garlic
1/4 tsp. onion powder
1/8 tsp. salt
1/8 tsp. pepper

In a large bowl, whisk together mayonnaise, sour cream, dried chives, dried parsley flakes, dried dillweed, ground garlic, onion powder, salt and pepper. Mix well and use as a dip for chicken wings or various cut vegetables. Will keep for 7 to 10 days in the refrigerator.

Beach Babe

Makes 1 serving

3/4 oz. scotch   3/4 oz. grapefruit juice
3/4 oz. dry vermouth

 In a cocktail shaker filled with ice, combine scotch, dry vermouth and grapefruit juice. Shake vigorously and strain into a highball glass.

Hole in One

Makes 1 serving

1 3/4 oz. scotch   1/4 tsp. lemon juice
3/4 oz. dry vermouth   Dash of orange bitters

 In a cocktail shaker filled with ice, combine scotch, dry vermouth, lemon juice and orange bitters. Shake vigorously and strain into a highball glass.

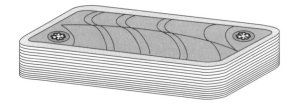

A ♣

Slow Cooked Meatballs

Makes 8 servings

2 lb. lean ground beef
1/4 C. water
1 small onion, minced
2 eggs, beaten
1 C. dry breadcrumbs
1 tsp. salt

1 (1 lb.) can cranberry sauce
1 (12 oz.) bottle chili sauce
2 T. brown sugar
1 T. lemon juice

In a large bowl, combine ground beef, water, minced onion, beaten eggs, dry breadcrumbs and salt. Mix by hand until well incorporated and shape into bite-sized meatballs. In a large saucepan over medium high heat, combine cranberry sauce, chili sauce, brown sugar and lemon juice. Heat mixture, stirring constantly, for about 4 minutes. Add uncooked meatballs to sauce mixture and stir until coated. Cover saucepan and let simmer for 1 hour. Before serving, transfer meatballs and sauce to a warm serving bowl, skimming the grease off the sauce. Encourage guests to enjoy meatballs, using toothpicks to remove from the bowl.

Garden Salsa

Makes 3 cups

1 medium green pepper, chopped
2 celery stalks, chopped
1 medium tomato, diced
1 small onion, chopped
1 medium carrot, chopped
1/4 C. fresh chopped cilantro

1 (14 1/2 oz.) can diced tomatoes, drained
1/2 C. water
1/2 C. tomato sauce
1/3 C. tomato paste
3 cloves garlic, minced
1 T. lemon juice
1/4 tsp. pepper

In a large bowl, combine chopped green pepper, chopped celery, diced tomato, chopped onion, chopped carrot and fresh chopped cilantro. In a separate bowl, combine drained diced tomatoes, water, tomato sauce, tomato paste, minced garlic, lemon juice and pepper. Mix well. Add tomato sauce mixture to vegetable mixture, stirring until well blended. Serve with tortilla chips for dipping.

A
♣

Roulette

Makes 1 serving

2 oz. gin
2 dashes orange bitters
1/4 tsp. maraschino
   liqueur

1/4 tsp. lemon juice
Ice cubes
1 maraschino cherry
   for garnish

In a cocktail shaker filled with ice, combine gin, orange bitters, maraschino liqueur and lemon juice. Shake vigorously and strain into a highball glass over ice. Garnish with a maraschino cherry.

Fog Horn

Makes 1 serving

Ice cubes
1 1/2 oz. gin
Juice of 1/2 lime

Ginger ale
Slice of lime for garnish

Fill a lowball glass with ice cubes. Pour gin and lime juice over ice and add ginger ale to fill glass. Mix lightly and garnish with a slice of lime.

A ♣ Pizza Quesadillas

Makes 8 servings

2 T. margarine, softened
8 (10") flour tortillas
1 (16 oz.) pkg. shredded
    Cheddar Monterey
    Jack cheese blend

1/2 C. pizza sauce
4 oz. sliced pepperoni

Spread margarine over one side of each tortilla. In a large skillet over medium low heat, place one tortilla, buttered side down. Spoon 1 tablespoon pizza sauce over half of the tortilla and sprinkle some of the shredded cheese blend over pizza sauce. Place a few pepperoni slices over cheese. Fold tortilla over to cover pizza fillings. When one side is golden brown, carefully flip over tortilla and cook other side until golden brown. Repeat with remaining tortillas and ingredients.

Brandy Alexander

Makes 1 serving

1 oz. dark crème de cacao
1 oz. brandy

Dash of half n' half
Nutmeg for garnish

In a cocktail shaker filled with ice, combine crème de cacao, brandy and half n' half. Shake vigorously and strain into a lowball glass over ice. Garnish with a dash of nutmeg.

Corkscrew

Makes 1 serving

1 1/2 oz. rum
1/2 oz. peach brandy

1/2 oz. dry vermouth
Lime wedge for garnish

In a cocktail shaker filled with ice, combine rum, peach brandy and dry vermouth. Shake vigorously and strain into a highball glass over ice. Garnish with a lime wedge.

A♣

Burger Bites

Makes 12 servings

3 slices white bread
2 T. butter, melted
6 oz. ground beef
1 green onion, minced
1/2 tsp. French mustard
1/2 tsp. Worcestershire
   sauce

Salt and pepper to taste
1/4 C. minced
   mushrooms
2 3/4 oz. crumbled
   blue cheese
Mayonnaise

Preheat oven to 375°. Using a small round biscuit cutter or knife, cut bread slices into 12 (1 1/2") rounds and place on a baking sheet. Brush melted butter over each bread round and bake in oven for 15 minutes, until golden brown. Meanwhile, in a small bowl, combine ground beef, minced green onion, French mustard, Worcestershire sauce, salt and pepper. Mix until well combined and shape mixture into 12 small burger patties. Place remaining melted butter in a medium saucepan over medium heat. Place minced mushrooms in saucepan and sauté until softened. Add burgers to saucepan and cook on each side for 2 to 3 minutes. Top each burger with some of the sautéed mushrooms and crumbled blue cheese. Spread a little mayonnaise over each mini bun and place one mini burger on each bun.

Mini Reubens

Makes 24 servings

1 1/2 C. processed sliced corned beef, chopped
1 C. sauerkraut, drained
1/2 C. shredded Swiss cheese

1/2 C. Thousand Island dressing
1 loaf thin rye bread slices

Preheat oven to 375°. In a medium bowl, combine chopped corned beef, drained sauerkraut, shredded Swiss cheese and Thousand Island dressing. Mix until well blended. Place a generous amount of the corned beef mixture over each rye bread slice. Place mini sandwiches on a baking sheet and bake in oven for 10 to 12 minutes, until cheese is melted. Remove from oven and serve warm.

Hop Frog

Makes 1 serving

3/4 oz. light rum   3/4 oz. apricot brandy
Juice of 1/2 lime   Ice cubes

In a cocktail shaker filled with ice, combine light rum, lime juice and apricot brandy. Shake vigorously and strain into a highball glass over ice.

Red Rider

Makes 1 serving

1 oz. bourbon   Ice cubes
1/2 oz. triple sec   Dash of grenadine
1 oz. lemon juice

In a cocktail shaker filled with ice, combine bourbon, triple sec and lemon juice. Shake vigorously and strain into a highball glass over ice. Add grenadine and serve.

A♣ Jalapeno Poppers

Makes 25 servings

12 oz. cream cheese,
    softened
1 (8 oz.) pkg. shredded
    Monterey Pepper
    Jack cheese blend
25 jalapeno peppers,
    seeded and halved

1 C. milk
1 C. flour
1 C. dry breadcrumbs
Oil for frying

In a medium bowl, combine cream cheese and Monterey Pepper Jack cheese blend, mixing until well combined. In a large pot of lightly salted simmering water over medium heat, place halved jalapeno peppers for 2 minutes. Drain peppers and thoroughly dry with paper towels. Spoon an even amount of the cream cheese mixture into each jalapeno half. Place milk, flour and dry breadcrumbs in separate shallow bowls. Dip the stuffed jalapenos first in the milk, then in the flour and then in the breadcrumbs, turning until well coated. Let jalapenos dry for about 10 minutes on paper towels, then dip again into the milk and roll again in breadcrumbs. Let dry and repeat until jalapenos are completely coated in breadcrumbs. In a medium skillet over high heat, heat oil to 365°. Carefully place a few stuffed jalapenos in hot oil, frying for 2 to 3 minutes on each side, until golden brown. Remove and let drain on paper towels. Repeat with remaining stuffed jalapenos.

A ♣ Fried Dill Pickles

Makes 12 to 16 servings

2 eggs, beaten
2 1/4 C. flour, divided
1 C. milk
1 T. Worcestershire sauce
1/2 tsp. hot sauce
1/4 tsp. seasoned salt
1/4 tsp. garlic powder
3/4 tsp. cayenne pepper

1 C. cornmeal
3/4 tsp. pepper
1 qt. sliced dill pickles,
   drained
Oil for frying
Salt and additional
   pepper to taste

In a medium bowl, combine beaten eggs, 1/4 cup flour, milk, Worcestershire sauce, hot sauce, seasoned salt, garlic powder and cayenne pepper. Mix well. In a separate bowl, combine cornmeal, remaining 2 cups flour and pepper. Dip drained pickles first into the milk mixture and then dredge in cornmeal mixture until well coated. In a medium skillet over high heat, heat oil to 350°. Carefully place a few coated pickles in hot oil, frying until pickles float to the top and are golden brown. Remove and let drain on paper towels. Season with salt and pepper to taste.

Treat all the girls to a night of poker – ladies only! Serve up some party themed foods, sweet cocktails and charming desserts... then take each other for all you've got!

Ladies Night Out

A ♦

Watermelon Pucker Smucker

Makes 1 serving

2 oz. watermelon pucker
2 oz. sprite

2 oz. orange juice
Twist of lime for garnish

Fill a highball glass with ice cubes. Pour watermelon pucker over ice and add sprite and orange juice. Mix lightly and garnish with a twist of lime.

Fruity Tootie

Makes 1 serving

5 oz. light rum
5 oz. coconut and
    pineapple nectar
5 oz. passion fruit juice

Ice cubes
Fresh pineapple
    chunk for garnish

In a blender, combine light rum, coconut and pineapple nectar and passion fruit juice. Pulse for 10 to 15 seconds, until well combined. Add desired amount of ice cubes and process on high until well blended. Pour into a Collins glass and garnish with a fresh pineapple chunk.

Strawberry Alexander

Makes 1 serving

5 oz. frozen sliced
   strawberries in syrup
1 scoop vanilla ice cream
1 oz. white crème de cacao
1 oz. brandy

Whipped topping for
   garnish
Chocolate shavings for
   garnish

In a blender, combine strawberries in syrup, vanilla ice cream, white crème de cacao and brandy. Blend until smooth and pour into a chilled Collins glass. Garnish with whipped topping and chocolate shavings.

Orange Cream Cocktail

Makes 1 serving

Ice Cubes
1 1/2 oz. vanilla Schnapps

1/4 C. orange juice
1 orange wedge for garnish

Fill a highball glass with ice cubes. Pour vanilla Schnapps over ice and add orange juice. Mix lightly and garnish with an orange wedge.

A
♦ Ace of Diamonds Cake

Makes 12 servings

1/2 C. buttermilk
1 tsp. baking soda
1/2 C. shortening
2 C. sugar
3 egg yolks
1 egg
1 tsp. vanilla
2 C. flour

1/2 tsp. salt
1 tsp. baking powder
1 C. boiling water
1 (16 oz.) tub creamy
   white frosting
1 (.68 oz.) tube red or
   black decorator's gel

Preheat oven to 350°. In a medium bowl, combine buttermilk and baking soda. Mix well and set aside. In a large bowl, cream together shortening, sugar, egg yolks, eggs and vanilla. Mix until lightened and fluffy and stir in buttermilk mixture. Into a separate bowl, sift flour, salt and baking powder. Add to creamed mixture and stir in boiling water. Pour batter in a greased and floured 9x13" baking dish. Bake in oven for about 35 minutes, or until a toothpick inserted in center of cake comes out clean. Remove from oven and let cool completely. Once cake has cooled, transfer cake to a serving platter and spread creamy white frosting over top and sides of cake. Use red or black decorator's gel to decorate cake like your favorite playing card.

Cherry Tarts

Makes 2 dozen

1 (8 oz.) pkg. refrigerated
    crescent rolls
1 (3 oz.) pkg. cream
    cheese, softened

1/4 C. powdered sugar
1 C. cherry pie filling
1/4 tsp. almond extract

Preheat oven to 375°. On a lightly floured surface, roll out crescent roll dough, pinching together seams to make one sheet. Cut dough into 2" circles. Press one circle into bottom and up sides of 24 miniature muffin cups. In a small mixing bowl, beat cream cheese and powdered sugar at medium speed until smooth. Place 1/2 teaspoon of the cream cheese mixture over dough in each muffin cup. In a separate bowl, combine cherry pie filling and almond extract. Place about 2 teaspoons of the cherry filling mixture over cream cheese mixture in each muffin cup. Bake in oven for 12 to 14 minutes, or until edges are lightly browned. Remove from oven and let cool on a wire rack. Chill in refrigerator until ready to serve.

A

Cran-Strawberry Cooler

Makes 4 servings

1 1/3 C. cranberry juice
2/3 C. white grape juice
10 fresh whole
    strawberries, hulled,
    divided

4 ice cubes
1/2 tsp. sugar, optional

In a blender, combine cranberry juice, white grape juice, 6 whole strawberries and ice. If desired, add sugar. Process on high until well blended. Pour mixture evenly into 4 chilled Collins glasses and garnish each serving with one of the remaining whole strawberries.

Lemon Pineapple Fizz

Makes 2 servings

1 (6 oz.) can pineapple
    juice, chilled
1 C. vanilla ice cream
1/2 C. lemon sherbet

1 to 2 drops yellow food
    coloring, optional
1 C. lemon lime soda,
    chilled

In a blender, combine pineapple juice, vanilla ice cream, lemon sherbet and, if desired, yellow food coloring. Process on high until well blended and smooth. Pour mixture evenly into 2 chilled Collins glasses and add 1/2 cup lemon lime soda to each glass. Mix lightly and serve.

A

A ♦

Grasshopper Pie

Makes 1 (9") pie

2 (3 oz.) pkgs. cream
  cheese, softened
1 (14 oz.) can sweetened
  condensed milk
15 drops green food
  coloring
24 chocolate-covered
  mint cookies, divided

2 C. whipped topping
1/2 T. crème de menthe
  liqueur
1 (9") prepared Oreo
  cookie crust

In a large mixing bowl, beat cream cheese until lightened and fluffy. Gradually beat in sweetened condensed milk, mixing until smooth. Add food coloring and mix well. Mixture should be light green. Coarsely crush 16 chocolate-covered mint cookies and fold into cream cheese mixture. Mix in whipped topping and crème de menthe liqueur. Pour mixture into prepared Oreo cookie pie crust and spread evenly. Cover and chill in freezer for 8 hours or overnight. Remove from freezer 15 minutes before serving and garnish with remaining 8 chocolate-covered mint cookies.

A
◆ Cookie Fruit Pizza

Makes 8 to 10 servings

1 (18 oz.) pkg. refrigerated
    sugar cookie dough
3/4 C. sugar
1 tsp. lemon juice
2 (8 oz.) pkgs. cream
    cheese, softened

1/2 C. sliced bananas
1/2 C. sliced fresh
    strawberries
1/2 C. sliced kiwi
1/2 C. seedless grapes,
    halved

Preheat oven to 350°. Press cookie dough evenly onto a greased 12" pizza pan. Bake in oven for 15 to 20 minutes, until golden brown. Meanwhile, in a large bowl, combine sugar, lemon juice and cream cheese. Remove cookie crust from oven and cool on a wire rack. Spread cream cheese mixture over cooled cookie. Arrange sliced fruit in a decorative pattern over cream cheese mixture. Chill in refrigerator until ready to serve.

Paradise Mixer

Makes 1 serving

2 1/2 oz. pineapple
  Schnapps
2 Boppin' Berry flavored
  Hi-C drinks

1 1/2 oz. Malibu rum
Dash of orange juice

In a highball glass filled with ice, pour pineapple Schnapps and Hi-C drinks. Stir just lightly and add rum. Mix well and add a dash of orange juice.

Fruity Toad

Makes 1 serving

1 oz. peach Schnapps
1 oz. triple sec

1 oz. lemon lime soda
Dash of 7-up soda

In a cocktail shaker filled with ice, combine peach Schnapps, triple sec, lemon lime soda and 7-up. Shake vigorously and strain into a chilled cocktail glass.

A
♦

White Chocolate Cranberry Pear Pastry

Makes 10 servings

1 egg, beaten
1 T. water
1 (17 1/4 oz.) pkg. frozen
    puffy pastry, thawed
1 (6 oz.) pkg. white
    baking chocolate

2 (15 oz.) cans sliced
    pears, drained
1/4 C. dried cranberries

Preheat oven to 375°. In a small bowl, combine beaten egg and water. Unfold pastry sheets on a lightly floured flat surface and trim about 1" off the corner of each pastry sheet, reserving trimmings. Place 1 pastry on an ungreased baking sheet. Chop 4 squares of the white baking chocolate into small pieces. In a medium bowl, combine chopped white chocolate, pears and cranberries. Spread mixture into the center of pastry on baking sheet to within 1" of the edges of the pastry. Brush edges of pastry with egg mixture. Top with remaining pastry sheet, press edges together with a fork to seal. If desired, decorate pastry with reserved pastry trimmings. Brush egg mixture over pastry. Cut slits, 2" apart, in top pastry crust. Bake in oven for 35 minutes or until pastry is golden brown. Let cool for about 30 minutes on a wire rack. In a double boiler, melt remaining 2 squares white baking chocolate. Drizzle melted white chocolate over pastry. Cut into squares or wedges to serve.

♦

A

A
◆ Poker Chip Cookies

Makes 2 dozen

3/4 C. shortening	2 1/2 C. flour
1/2 C. sugar	1 tsp. baking powder
2 eggs	1 tsp. salt
1 tsp. vanilla	1 T. dry cherry gelatin

Preheat oven to 400°. In a medium bowl, cream together shortening, sugar, eggs and vanilla. Mix well and stir in flour, baking powder and salt. Mix well until a stiff dough forms. Set aside all but 3/4 cup of the dough. To the 3/4 cup dough, mix in dry cherry gelatin until dough is red, adding more gelatin if needed. Roll out red dough into a 7 1/2" by 9" rectangle. Roll out 3/4 cup of the white dough into a 7 1/2" by 9" rectangle. Cut rectangles, lengthwise, into 7 (1") strips. Assemble two rectangles by placing strips next to each other in alternating colors. Use 7 strips for each rectangle. Lightly pinch seams together and press gently so strips form two solid rectangles. Roll remaining white dough into logs that are 2" in diameter and 9" long. Place one dough log along the side of each striped rectangle. Carefully roll dough so striped dough rectangle makes a layer around dough log. Press gently to close the long seam. Cut dough into 1/4" to 1/2" slices and place face down on ungreased baking sheets. Cookies should look like poker chips. Bake in oven for 8 to 10 minutes, or until cookies are lightly browned. Remove from oven and let cool on a wire rack.

A ♦ Mock Champagne Punch

Makes 8 to 10 servings

2/3 C. sugar
2/3 C. water
1 C. grapefruit juice
1/2 C. orange juice

3 T. grenadine syrup
1 (28 oz.) bottle
   ginger ale, chilled

In a medium saucepan over low heat, combine sugar and water. Mix well, until sugar is completely dissolved. Bring mixture to a boil for 10 minutes. Remove from heat and let cool. Mix in grapefruit juice and orange juice. Chill in refrigerator. To serve, place mixture in a punch bowl and stir in grenadine and chilled ginger ale.

Chocolate Cake Shooter

Makes 1 shot

1 oz. hazelnut liqueur   1 lemon wedge
1/2 oz. vodka   Sugar

Into a shot glass, pour hazelnut liqueur and vodka. Coat lemon wedge with sugar. To drink, suck on sugar coated lemon wedge and shoot the drink. Should taste just like chocolate cake in your mouth!

B-52 Shooter

Makes 2 shots

1 (1 1/2 oz.) jigger Irish   1 (1 1/2 oz.) jigger dark
   cream liqueur   crème de cacao

In a cocktail shaker or glass, combine Irish cream liqueur and crème de cacao. Shake or stir and pour evenly into 2 shot glasses. If desired, may substitute 1 1/2 ounces Kahlua for jigger of crème de cacao.

Absolute Fruit Martini

Makes 1 serving

1/2 oz. banana flavored liqueur

1/2 oz. watermelon flavored liqueur

1/2 oz. vodka

In a cocktail shaker filled with ice, combine banana liqueur, watermelon liqueur and vodka. Shake vigorously and strain into a chilled martini glass.

Red Hottie

Makes 1 serving

Ice cubes

1 oz. tequila

3/4 oz. amaretto

Pineapple juice

1 oz. grenadine syrup

1 maraschino cherry

Fill a Collins glass with ice cubes. Pour tequila and amaretto over ice and add pineapple juice to fill glass. Mix lightly and top with grenadine syrup. Garnish with a maraschino cherry.

A ♦ Caramel Surprise Cupcakes

Makes 2 dozen

1 (18 1/4 oz.) chocolate cake mix	3/4 C. chocolate chips
24 caramels	1 C. chopped walnuts
	Chocolate frosting, optional

Preheat oven to 350°. In a large mixing bowl, prepare cake mix according to package directions. Line 24 muffin cups with paper liners and fill each cup 1/3 full with chocolate batter. Set remaining batter aside. Bake in oven for 7 to 8 minutes, or until top of cupcakes appear to be set. Gently press one caramel into each cupcake and sprinkle some of the chocolate chips and chopped walnuts over caramel in each cupcake. Divide remaining batter evenly over filling in each cupcake. Return to oven for an additional 15 to 20 minutes, or until top of cupcakes spring back when lightly touched. Remove from oven and let cool in pan for 5 minutes. Remove to wire racks to cool completely. If desired, frost cupcakes with chocolate frosting before serving.

Lemonade Strawberry Slush

Makes 4 servings

1 (10 oz.) pkg. frozen
   sliced strawberries,
   thawed
3/4 C. pink lemonade
   concentrate

3/4 C. water
3/4 C. ice cubes
1 C. club soda

In a blender, combine sliced strawberries, pink lemonade concentrate, water and ice cubes. Process on high until well blended and smooth. Pour mixture into a plastic freezer container, cover and place in freezer at least 12 hours. Before serving, let mixture stand at room temperature for 1 hour. Stir in club soda and divide mixture evenly into 4 Collins glasses.

A

◆ Macadamia Cocoa Cookies

Makes 2 1/2 dozen

3/4 C. butter or
    margarine, softened
1/2 C. powdered sugar
1/3 C. sugar
1 tsp. vanilla

1 C. flour
1/2 C. cocoa powder
2/3 C. chopped
    macadamia nuts

Preheat oven to 350°. In a medium bowl, cream together butter, powdered sugar and sugar. Mix until lightened and fluffy and stir in vanilla. In a separate bowl, combine flour and cocoa powder. Gradually add flour mixture to butter mixture and stir until well combined. Fold in chopped macadamia nuts. Shape dough into 1 1/2" balls and place 2" apart on ungreased baking sheets. Flatten cookies with a fork and bake in oven for 12 to 14 minutes, or until the surface of the dough cracks. Remove from oven and let cool slightly on baking sheets before transferring to wire racks.

A ♦

Irish Cream
Cappuccino Cocktail

Makes 1 serving

1 oz. Irish cream liqueur
1/4 oz. white crème de
  cacao

1/4 oz. Kahlua
1 oz. milk

In a cocktail shaker filled with ice, combine Irish cream liqueur, white crème de cacao, Kahlua and milk. Shake vigorously, until frothy and strain into a chilled martini glass.

Caribbean Dream

Makes 1 serving

1 1/2 oz. light rum
1 oz. amaretto
2 oz. pineapple juice
2 oz. orange juice

Dash of grenadine syrup
1 orange slice for garnish
1 pineapple slice for
  garnish

In a cocktail shaker filled with ice, combine light rum, amaretto, pineapple juice and orange juice. Shake vigorously and strain into a chilled cocktail glass. Add a dash of grenadine and garnish with an orange and pineapple slice.

Creamy Peanut Butter Pie

Makes 1 (9") pie

1 (8 oz.) pkg. cream
   cheese, softened
1/2 C. sugar
1/3 C. creamy peanut
   butter

1/3 C. whipped topping
10 peanut butter cups
1 (9") prepared Oreo
   cookie crust

In a small mixing bowl, beat cream cheese, sugar and peanut butter at medium speed until smooth. Fold in whipped topping. Coarsely chop half of the peanut butter cups and carefully fold chopped peanut butter cups into cream cheese mixture. Spoon mixture into Oreo cookie crust. Cut remaining half of the peanut butter cups into quarters and use to garnish top of pie. Chill in refrigerator at least 4 hours before cutting into slices and serving.

A

Frosted
Poker Cookies

Makes 4 1/2 dozen

2 C. butter, softened
1 3/4 C. sugar
1 egg yolk

4 C. flour
Prepared vanilla frosting
Food coloring

In a large mixing bowl, combine butter and sugar at low speed until well combined. Add egg yolk and beat until well mixed. Gradually add flour and mix by hand until a dough forms. Roll dough into 1" balls and place 2" apart on ungreased baking sheets. Place sugar in a shallow bowl. Dip bottom of glass in sugar and gently flatten each cookie. Bake in oven for 8 to 10 minutes, or until lightly browned. Remove from oven and let cool slightly on baking sheets before transferring to wire racks to cool. Decorate cookies like various poker-themed objects, such as poker chips, coins or a roulette table. Tint the vanilla frosting with the appropriate food coloring. Use a piping bag for more precise details.

A

◆ Tropical Parfaits

Makes 2 servings

2 C. cold milk
1 (3 1/2 oz.) pkg. instant
  coconut cream
  pudding mix
1 tsp. grated lime peel,
  optional
1/2 C. pineapple tidbits,
  drained

1/2 C. plus 1 T. sliced
  almonds, toasted*
1/2 C. fresh sliced
  strawberries
Whipped topping
2 maraschino cherries

In a medium bowl, beat together milk and coconut cream pudding mix with a wire whisk. Fold in grated lime peel. To assemble parfaits, divide about 1/3 of the pudding mixture in the bottom of each of two parfait glasses. Top each serving with 1/4 cup pineapple tidbits and 2 tablespoons toasted sliced almonds. Divide another 1/3 of the pudding mixture into each glass and top each with 1/4 cup sliced strawberries and another 2 tablespoons toasted sliced almonds. Top each serving with the remaining pudding mixture and remaining toasted almonds. Top parfaits with a dollop of whipped topping and garnish each serving with one maraschino cherry.

*To toast, place sliced almonds on a baking sheet. Bake at 350° for approximately 10 minutes or until almonds are golden brown.

A

Purple Gecko

Makes 1 serving

1 1/2 oz. tequila
1/2 oz. blue curacao
1/2 oz. red curacao
1 oz. cranberry juice

1 1/2 oz. lemon lime soda
1/2 oz. lime juice
Sugar or salt

In a cocktail shaker filled with ice, combine tequila, blue curacao, red curacao, cranberry juice, lemon lime soda and lime juice. Dip the rim of a margarita glass in sugar or salt. Shake drink mixture vigorously and strain into prepared margarita glass.

Strawberry Margarita on the Rocks

Makes 1 serving

1 oz. tequila
1/2 oz. triple sec
1 oz. strawberry Schnapps
1 oz. lime juice

1 oz. fresh sliced
     strawberries
Sugar
Ice cubes

In a cocktail shaker filled with ice, combine tequila, triple sec, strawberry Schnapps, lime juice and fresh sliced strawberries. Dip the rim of a margarita glass in sugar. Shake drink mixture vigorously and strain into prepared margarita glass. Add ice.

A

The Best Strawberry Tarts

Makes 6 servings

4 oz. cream cheese,
    softened
1/4 C. sugar
2 1/4 tsp. milk
1 1/2 tsp. sour cream

1/2 tsp. vanilla
6 individual graham
    cracker tart shells
1 1/2 C. sliced strawberries
1 C. strawberry glaze

In a small mixing bowl, beat cream cheese, sugar, milk, sour cream and vanilla at medium speed, until well combined. Spoon mixture evenly into graham cracker tart shells. In a separate bowl, combine sliced strawberries and strawberry glaze. Mix well and spoon mixture over cream cheese filling in each tart. Chill in refrigerator until ready to serve.

A ♦

Rhubarb Dream Bars

Makes about 2 dozen

1 1/4 C. flour, divided
1/3 C. powdered sugar
1/2 C. butter or
   margarine, cold
1 1/4 C. sugar

2 eggs
2 C. finely chopped
   rhubarb
1/2 C. chopped walnuts
1/2 C. shredded coconut

Preheat oven to 350°. In a medium bowl, combine 1 cup flour and powdered sugar. Using a pastry blender, cut in butter until mixture is crumbly. Press mixture evenly into bottom of a lightly greased 9x13" baking dish. Bake in oven for 13 to 15 minutes, until edges are lightly browned. In a large bowl, combine remaining 1/4 cup flour, sugar and eggs. Mix until well combined and fold in chopped rhubarb, chopped walnuts and shredded coconut. Pour mixture over baked crust layer in baking dish and return to oven for an additional 30 to 35 minutes, until set. Remove from oven and let cool on a wire rack before cutting into bars.

Index

All About Poker

Poker Card Games

Amateur Night

For High Rollers Only

Down & Dirty Party

Ladies Night Out